PUCKLIE O' PICKLES

A selection of Scots yarns

Compiled by
A J Stovie

ISBN: 9798680037805
Independently published

Book cover design by yerai ibarria

facebook.com/ajstovie
twitter.com/ajstovie

To Geordie, a loyal
and loving companion.

Contents

Acknowledgements

A huge thank you to book-writing course coach Val Scouten for her advice, patience, tips and encouragement and for providing an environment which cultures friendship with fellow writers. Also, appreciation to the Zoom book team crew during Lockdown which instigated some of the stories included in *Pucklie O' Pickles; A selection of Scots yarns*.

Sincere gratitude to good friends for reviewing samples from the book and offering invaluable feedback and for the love and patience from family members who muffled their boredom as they heard these stories over and over again.

Finally, but not least, loving thanks to all partners of aspiring writers who quietly persevere the unsociable writing stints - rising with the lark and burning the midnight oil - but who always stalwartly provide their unwavering support, sometimes with a welcome cup of tea.

Prologue

We all experience a dilemma, an uninvited predicament or conundrum, at some point in our lives. It may be just a passing hiccup or a serious disruption; self-inflicted or consequence of the actions by others or the environment; financial, emotional, moral, ethical or merely circumstantial.

It's the disparity between our expectations and the reality of outcomes that brings us that unexpected surprise or disappointment. Unfortunately, if a situation spirals outwith our control, heartbreak or stress to varying degree may ensue.

We may always strive to make sensible decisions in life's path but, sadly, on occasion, like a *spiders web of pickles* there may be long lasting unintentional consequences, not only to ourselves but to others.

It's a lang road that's no goat a turnin'

*(Don't lose heart in dark times,
things can't keep going
in the same direction forever)*

A J Stovie

.

Sandra McFadyen's Bestie Jane Fonda

Straining her neck, Sandra lifted her head off the stale smelling rug and twisted it towards her TV screen.

'Yes. Can you feel the burn? Hold it. Hold it. 5, 4, 3, …'

'Oh aye. Jeez, ah can feel it burnin' Jane. Ma wee leg's fair shooglin' wi' it. Can ah put it doon noo?'

'Well done ladies. Let's stretch out. Cool down.'

Sandra rolled on to all fours grunting and puffing as she struggled to stand up.

'Stretch your arms up and sweep them down. That's it, and again, great, and once more...

…stretch up…fantastic! Long breath out. Thank you and well done for staying with me to the end. Goodbye until next time.'

'Wait Jane, d'you have to go?' Rubbing her aching hip, Sandra paused the video, freezing the image on the screen.

'Ah was kinda hopin' you would stay for a wee natter. Ah dinnae mind tellin' you, since this so-called lock-doon started ah've been gie lonely. Ah've hardly spoken tae a soul in months.

Mind you, ah wiznae seein' many folk before all of this debacle, except the young couple across the landing, Jennifer and Patrick. They're good tae me mind but they just leave ma' messages ootside ma' door wi' hardly a word.

Och. An ah'm missing my wee blethers and cuppas wi' Duncan doon the stairs. He's a right auld sweetie, Jane. That man never missed a trick. He kent a'thing aboot a'body in the stair. Ah'd invite him up here but they're sayin' us auld yins huv tae stay away fae everybody else.

That's why, ah've been fair enjoyin' oor wee mornin' sessions together, Jane. Ah'm chuffed ah found you in that box of old videos, at the back of the glory hole in the back bedroom. *Jane Fonda's Complete Body Work Out 1982!* Nooadays ye might be a wee bit frayed aroond the edges but you've worn better than me. Ah kept my video player when everybody was tossing theirs oot. Ah never throw anything away Jane. You just dinnae ken when it'll come in handy, dae ye? Like now?

This might sound crazy Jane but ah always thought you and me had a lot in common. Ah was a 'right-on' wee radge in the 60's. A feminist and activist just like you, Jane. If there wis anything getting banned, you could bet your life ah'd be out shoutin' the odds! Aye, ah was always one for standin' up fur women, fighting fur human rights and defending the underdog. Been a Socialist a' ma' days. Staunch like. Maybe no such a firebrand nowadays but ah still rattle their cages. Ah write blisterin' letters to that useless Tory government an' oor numpty councillors. Ah complain aboot thay lazy bloody bin-men and the state o' the streets. F***ing disgraceful.

An' the trams! Och dinnae get me started. Ah never get a reply mind, but it gies me a wee walk doon tae the post box.

We've seen the world go through pretty hairy times, eh Jane? But ah never imagined in ma' puff anythin' like this plague comin'. Did you?

By the way, ah read your book. When you came oot admitting tae stickin yer finger doon yer throat tae puke up after eatin', tae stay skinny. Ah didnae judge you Jane. Ah wish ah'd made ma'self puke up some o' they many fish suppers. An' you had issues wi' yer old man? Well there's somethin' else we huv in common. Ah hated ma' big bastard of a faither. Drunken auld sod. Made my mam's life a misery. Christ, could you imagine bein' in lock-doon wi' that evil psycho?

Since it's only you an' me here Jane, and ah'll whisper this confidentially, an' ah know it won't go any further, ah'll let you into a secret.

When ah wiz in ma' teens, ah came hame one day to find my Mam had fled an' the bastardin' swine wis lyin' drunk on the kitchen floor choking on his own vomit. Ah just turned around and ah quietly let myself oot. Ah took a long, slow walk aroond the block twice.

When ah got hame, he was deid. The doctor wrote on the death certificate, *'Death by misadventure.'*

Ah huv nae bad conscience or regrets aboot that day, Jane.

Och Jane, it's done me good chattin' tae you. Same time tomorrow eh?

Ah'm gan' ben tae put the kettle on and sit at the front window wi' a nice mug o' tea an' watch the world go by. Nae many folk in the streets tae watch nooadays. All too feart o' the dreaded C virus, tae venture oot.

Ah, but ah forgot. Today's bucket day! The binmen'll be comin'. Where's ma specs an' writing pad…?'

Mad March Hare

A few years back, while sipping a welcome morning coffee, I picked up the previous day's *Scotsman* which was lying on the breakfast table. Giving it a cursory browse, I noticed a small article hidden away on page 4. I think I registered it because Arran featured in the title.

As a child, I have many happy memories of spending family holidays, comfortably ensconced in the lovely Mrs Adams Guest House which was located only a stone's throw away from the beach on Lamlash's wide sweeping bay. Fourteen halcyon sun-lit carefree days every summer. And no school. Bliss!

As I read through the article, I shook the paper with an exclamation of outrage.

'God in Heaven! Have you seen this?'

My husband eyed me with quiet curiosity, from across the table.

'…Where's your specs? Och, I'll read it out to you. Listen to this! Unbelievable!'

> *'A tenant farmer, Mr Jon Gillies, whose family have resided and worked a small holding farm in Brodick on the Isle of Arran for the past century, has been informed, by his landlord, he is to be evicted from the property on the 31st March of this month. The landowner has so far given no reasonable explanation. An appeal has been lodged with the Scottish Parliament and a demonstration of support for Mr Gillies and his family is scheduled to take place on the morning of 29th March….'*

I read no further. 'That's **today**? Right! Get your coat! We're going up there **now**!'

After parking the car at Holyrood, we joined a gathering placard-waving crowd all hyped up to commence their protest march, up towards Parliament. Falling into step with them, I started conversation with a young lad, a hippy, who periodically shouted into a megaphone. It sounded to me like, 'STOP THE CULL!'

'Hmmm, yeah,' I vigorously nodded to him in agreement.

'I suppose it could be seen like that. Bloody ruling-class bastards don't see us as human beings, do they? When I read about the eviction I just had to come. You have to try to do **something,** to stop this kind of thing, don't you?'

He momentarily took a rest from his chant then fired himself up again.

'The population will continue to be put at risk by wealthy land-owners intent on protecting their bloody grouse shooting estates. The notion of voluntary restraint is just being ignored,' he jabbered with pressing compassion and in earnest. He shook his head in disgust. 'The Scottish Government needs to do more to protect these endangered species.'

'Endangered species?' I puzzled on his choice of words whilst thinking it an unusual way to describe the working class.

As we took our stance on the Piazza, on the frontage of the Scottish Parliament building, I felt a nudge as I was forcefully pushed aside.

'Let me through, please…,' a firm voice commanded from behind.

As I turned to give way, I blinked in surprise. A giant man-size fluffy, white rabbit eased passed me as it was escorted for a press photo-shoot.

'What the heck's *that* about?' I uttered, turning to a woman standing next to me.

'Yeah, good isn't it?' she grinned. 'Since we're all here demonstrating to save the white mountain hares, we thought it would be a clever press gimmick. To have a hare spearheading the campaign shows they're properly represented.'

She clocked my confused expression.

'I'm sure if you ask, he'll let you take a selfie with him,' she joked.

The penny dropped.

'So, this demonstration is *not* about the eviction of a tenant farmer in Arran?' I frowned.

She shot me an odd glance.

'No' she retorted impatiently, as she crept away.

Waiting until after the crowd dispersed, I took her suggestion and sidled up to the monster fluffy hare for a selfie.

Yes, that was one Mad March Day when I got it embarrassingly wrong…but not completely.

As we were leaving, I noticed a young man awkwardly waiting at the Parliament entrance, surrounded by the probing press.

'Wait! It's him!' I alerted my husband.

Moving towards the young ruddy-faced farmer lad, I suddenly felt an acute rush of pity. There he stood, a big sturdy country youngster, bursting out of his badly fitting suit and fathoms out of his comfort zone. He was answering press questions politely about concern of his uncertain future.

'If this disnae get stopped today, me an' ma brither will be emptied oot o' the only hame wur family's ever known fur generations and a' oor possessions will be dumped outside tomorrow fur the sheriff's sale.'

Tears welled up in my eyes. I stepped forward, briefly attracting his attention.

'I know where you're coming from. I wish you the very best of luck. I'm genuinely sorry.' I felt completely lame.

As he turned his eyes on me, it came to me that he resembled a hopeless hare, caught in headlights.

'Thanks,' he muttered as he slunk away into the dim, cavernous Parliament building.

I read some days later, his appeal failed.

The Briny Sea

A 1960s Children's Story

As a child of nine, Edinburgh Waverley Station wasn't only about steam trains belching smoke or the newsagent kiosk where I'd choose comics to pass the journey, it was all about excitement. It meant summer holidays at Mrs Johnstone's lavender polished Guest House; it meant summer picnics on the beach; it meant the chip-van parked in Lamlash Bay and candy-floss and knickerbocker glories; it meant night time walks under a full harvest moon and all of the things I associated with our two-week annual holiday in Arran.

I sat on the station platform bench, wriggling my bottom impatient for us to be on our way. Jiggling my feet impatiently in my brand, new red Clark's sandals whilst admiring my gleaming white ankle socks and newly purchased C&A blue checked summer frock, I willed my cousins to appear.

'There they are!' my mum yelled.

She waved to my Aunty Betty who blew us kisses whilst Uncle Bill struggled with two heavy cases along the platform and my two cousins James and Maureen ran helter-skelter towards us. Of-course, the holiday didn't feel as if it had properly started until after we had boarded the train, settled into our seats, then passed through the long, long dark tunnel. My tummy flipped. *Hurrah! We we're on our way!*

Is it a cliché to say that all my memories of those summer holidays were of hot sunny days and blue skies? Well that's the way I remember them. Being an only child, I loved having the company of my cousins. I played mostly with my cousin James who was a year older than me. Maureen occasionally deigned to play cards with us but being a few years older, she usually stayed in the company of the adults. I would observe my mum roll her eyes to Aunty Betty when Maureen refused to get up in the mornings.

'Teenagers!' she shrugged. As if THAT explained everything.

In the morning, around the breakfast table over a big cooked breakfast, the adults made a plan for the day based on whether the little pink lady with her parasol or the little blue man under his umbrella showed themselves from the alpine house. The weather ornament forecasted the weather, *dry* or *wet*.

'It's going to be a sunny day!' my mother exclaimed, 'what does everyone want to do?'

Uncle Bill announced he had booked a round of golf. Auntie Betty and my mother were all for improving their sun-tans. My mother turned to my father.

'We'll take the kids down to the beach.'

'I think I'll take out one of the rowing boats for a day's fishing,' he decided.

'Can I come with you dad?' I begged. 'I've never been out on a boat, fishing.'

'Can I go too?' James piped up.

Aunty Betty shook her head at him. 'No, you can't go. You can't swim.'

'Pleeeeese, will you take me with you dad?' I clasped my hands in front of him in a plea gesture.

'Alright,' he agreed, 'glad to have your company Missy.'

As we left, I looked back to see James glaring daggers at me. I pulled a smug face at him as I skipped away at my dad's heels.

Raising my chin, I took in a breath of briny air, welcoming the cool sea breeze that blew through my hair, lifting it with the wind. I felt a frisson of excitement as we strolled around Brodick harbour, my jelly shoes slap-slapping along the hot surface of the pavement. This was going to be such a treat. The highlight of the whole holiday.

Holding my hand in a firm grip Dad guided me down the steep harbour steps to a little rowing boat bobbing at the quayside. Whilst he kept the little vessel steady for me, I clambered aboard and sat down amongst coiled ropes at the back of the boat, my nose wrinkling at the powerful smell of caught fish.

'Welcome aboard bosun,' dad said in a jokey voice.

He grasped the oars and dipping them into the water, he braced his feet against the sides ready to row backwards. Pulling back strongly, he propelled us out to the bumpy sea.

Sitting opposite him, my face was shaded from the bright sun by a wide brim straw hat. Trailing the tips of my fingers in the rippling water, I gazed down into its shifting green depths. Listening to the rhythmic splash of the oars as they carried us further and further out towards the straight line of the horizon. When the shoreline became a distant grey smudge, my dad brought the oars safely into the boat and began to attach bait to the hooks on the fishing lines. Pink worms, he had dug up earlier that morning from wet, wave-grooved sand, were pinned on.

'Here you go,' he instructed as he handed me a fishing line, 'do it like this.'

He flicked the rod back then using a quick wrist action, he swung the line forward landing the baited hook, just braking the surface of the water. With a little help, I cast my line and waited patiently for a fish to bite. A frothy ripple in the water made me cry out in excitement.

'Dad, look! There's a fish! Look there!' I pointed into the deep blue swirling water. A tug on my line confirmed it. I had a catch!

'Ste-ady! Don't jerk the line,' Dad cautioned. 'Just reel him in, nice and slow.'

'I've got him.' I held on to my rod tightly and as the fish pulled and fought for freedom, I reeled him in.

'Ah, ya beauty! Herring for supper!' Dad exclaimed, as the wriggling silver darling flopped around on the deck gasping for breath, the hook cruelly impaled in the roof of its gaping mouth. Its grey jelly-like eye was fixed on me. It was pleading with me for freedom.

'Let it go,' I cried. 'Dad, PLEASE let it go,' I wailed. 'I don't want to kill it. Please throw it back! NOW dad, NOW!' my cries heightened.

He looked at me in consternation but, shaking his head, he said, 'Alright, alright, calm down.'

Gripping the slippery fish, he unhooked it and threw it back into the ocean for freedom. Swooping gulls screeched and circled as my dad turned the boat around and rowed back towards the shore. I wept all the way back, my eyes turning red and my nose leaking snot.

James was kicking a ball against the wall when we got back.

'How many fish did you catch then?' he asked eagerly.

Fresh tears burst from my eyes. Dad raised his eyebrows and made a long face to James. Then he shrugged in bewilderment.

'*Women*,' he uttered. As if THAT explained everything.

Whenever I smell the briny sea, that day comes back to me with dewy-eyed nostalgia.

I've never eaten fish since.

A Good Heart

It was definitely not a good start that morning.

When Mrs Ferguson caught her on the stairs, Sadie McIntosh felt her stress levels rising.

'Morning Mrs Ferguson. How's things with you today?'

Sadie knew she didn't have time to stop and chat so she gave a quick smile and attempted her get-away but the old lady grasped on to her arm.

'I've been waiting for you Sadie,' she said in a wheezy voice, '…could you get a stair meeting organised? Those young lads who moved into the flat above me are throwing parties every night. I canny sleep for their music blaring… thud, thud, thud, thud…' She screwed her eyes shut.

'…and all sorts of guffies goin' in and oot,' she frowned. 'We need to get a haud of the landlord… This morning I had to mop the landing. Pee…' she wrinkled her nose. '…the dirty so and so's. I'm fair scunnered and ye ken the kind of language I get if I tackle them. Do you know, I caught one of them..'

Sadie interrupted her.

'Aye Mrs Ferguson, I canny sleep for their din either. Something'll have to be done. I'll go round the neighbours on Saturday and we'll organise a parle. We need to talk aboot that roof leak as well but I really have to go now or I'll miss my bus.'

'Aye. On ye go hen.' Mrs Ferguson released Sadie's arm remarking, 'Thank you dear. You've got a good heart. I know you'll see tae it, won't you Sadie?' Sadie nodded.

'Aye,' she thought, 'I'll see to it but why does it always have to be ME? Where will I find the money for a roof repair on the pittance I get paid? Suppose I'll have to break into my savings. I'm never going to get the wherewithal for that visit to my Raymond in Canada. I would have liked to see my wee brother before I get too old to make the trip.'

The No 12 drew up at the bus stop. If she put a spurt on, she might just catch it. She started to run but a sharp squeezing pain in her chest drew her up short. Rubbing her chest, she swore quietly under her breath.

'Bugger, missed it!'

She stood in the cold rain waiting for the next bus. Sod's law, it was late.

Before visiting her first client, she had to pick up shopping. A right old nippy sweety was Mrs Ogilvie-Smyth, AND don't forget that hyphen. Sadie couldn't get the brand of tea at Lidls that Mrs Ogilvie-Smyth always insisted on so she made a detour to Tesco. With a sinking heart, she was now 15 minutes late. Mrs Ogilvie-Smyth was a real stickler for punctuality and not only that, the community nurse had arranged to make a visit to speak with Sadie. She wouldn't be too happy if Sadie wasn't there to open the door. She'll probably report her.

Breathing heavily, a film of sweat forming on her brow from exertion, Sadie set down the heavy bag of shopping on the top step of the old lady's Victorian semi. Giving her shoulder a rub, she pondered a moment on whether at fifty-three she was getting too old to be lugging clients' heavy shopping bags. She scolded herself for not bringing her shopping-trolley but it was such a faff getting it on and off the bus. She rummaged in her shoulder bag for the door key and, making sure to wipe her feet, she let herself in to the cream carpeted hall.

With an air of disapproval, Sadie noticed layers of dust on the hall table and the carpet cleaning was much to be desired. Jodie was a local lass who Mrs Ogilvy-Smyth hired as a cleaner, but she often carelessly cut corners.

'Yes,' Sadie decided, 'she's a lazy besom.'

Once, she even caught Jodie, feet up on the sofa, flicking through a magazine.

'Just taking ma tea break,' said the shiftless skiver with a rebellious expression at being clocked.

Sadie would have a quiet word with her some-time. Maybe tomorrow when hopefully she'd turn up for work.

Whilst hanging up her coat on the hall-stand Sadie briefly checked herself in the mirror. She frowned. She didn't look too good. She needed a decent hair cut instead of the DIY chop she attempted - but hairdressing salons cost money. Too many convenience meals and fish suppers had given her an extra chin, but who has the time or energy to cook for one? Looking closer, she pondered that her skin was a strange colour and that purple tinge couldn't be normal. She would try to make time to arrange an appointment with the doctor. Get checked over.

'Maybe I'm going down with something,' she tutted, depositing the overflowing shopping bag on the kitchen table.

'Right brace yourself,' she muttered to herself before calling out in a cheery tone.

'Cooee!'

She popped her head round the bedroom door.

'Morning my lovely. How are we today?' she chirped.

Breezing over to draw back the curtains, she let a shaft of morning sun brighten the stale-smelling room.

'Sorry I'm late Mrs O. I missed the bus. I got properly chilled waiting for the next one. The good news is I got the tea you like, what is it called again, *lapsongsochong*? Shall I get you a cuppa before I get you up and dressed?'

Sadie checked her phone.

'Aye well maybe not, I've only got fifteen minutes with you till I have to leave to get to my next lady. Let's see how we get on.'

A muffled voice rasped at her from under the covers.

'I didn't get a blasted wink of sleep last night for the pain in my hip,' the wizened old lady groaned.

She surfaced and tried to raise herself up on her elbows but flopped back on the pillow.

'I'm exhausted.'

'No problem Mrs O. Here, let me help you.' Sadie slid her arm under the old lady's shoulders and *gie-in' it laldy*, she hauled her up.

'The community nurse is coming soon. We'll ask her if she can get something prescribed to help with the pain.'

Placing an extra pillow under the old lady's shoulders for support, she thought to herself, '*You wouldn't think such a rickle of bones could weigh so heavy. I should really ask them to provide a hoist.*'

Folding back the bedclothes, Sadie felt a sharp pain run down her arm.

Exhaling a long sigh, she thought, '*That's all I need. I've only gone and strained myself.*'

She called out raising her voice so that the hard-of-hearing Mrs Ogilvie-Smyth could hear.

'If you're alright to be left a couple of minutes Mrs O, I have to make a phone call to my supervisor. After that I'll get you breakfast. Tea and toast OK?'

Mrs Ogilvie-Smyth gave a haughty dismissive wave.

'If you must but I can't be kept waiting ALL morning.'

Whilst Sadie filled the kettle and put a couple of slices of toast under the grill she thought about the mean spirited old duffer.

She'd never had a kindly word from her in all of the fifteen years she'd been her carer. Sadie had a good heart though and wasn't one to dwell on the many slights she'd suffered from the curmudgeonly old woman. She pulled out her phone from her bag to make the call.

'Hello Effie. Look dear I canny make it to my next lady. Can you get her covered? I'm no feeling right at all and… eh? Yeah, I know you're short staffed but, honestly, I'm going to have to go home. Aye I know I'll get money docked off me but I canny help being sick, can I? Alright, alright calm doon. Don't get your knickers in a twist. I'll go.'

Sadie felt her blood pressure spiralling through the roof. Whilst her supervisor was still laying off to her on the need to be completely reliable, she interrupted the bollocking.

'I have to go. The toast's burning.' She hung up.

Mrs Ogilvie-Smyth's bell was ringing imperiously, an impatient summons. Sadie rolled her eyes.

'Holy heck, what does she want now?'

Keeping the harassed edge from her tone, she called, 'It's alright Mrs O, I'm just coming!'

At that moment, the burning toast under the grill billowed black smoke in the kitchen and it set off the smoke-alarm.

'Oh my God what the…,' Sadie panicked. She lifted the broom and stretching it up, she poked the end at the siren. But it didn't stop. The loud shrill, *beep, beep, beep,* carried on.

'Pipe down!' she pleaded.

'Ooof!' she shouted as she sat down heavily on the kitchen chair feeling nauseous and dizzy.

As the smoke alarm continued its *beep beep beep*, Mrs Ogilvie Smyth's bell was ringing louder and more persistent.

Standing up half-way to respond, Sadie then doubled over, clutching at her chest as a wave of pain ran along her jaw. It travelled down her neck into her shoulder and pressed down on her chest like a massive weight bearing down on her before slamming her to the ground.

'Oh god someone help me,' she slurred, lying helpless, engulfed in pain.

The front door bell's *buzz, buzz, buzzing* was the last thing she heard as she lost consciousness.

The community nurse acted quickly. When she couldn't get an answer and discovered black smoke seeping through the kitchen window, she rang the police who organised a lock-smith to break in and an ambulance was called. They found Mrs Ogilvie-Smyth dead, prostrate on her bedroom floor with a nasty gash on her fore-head. Apparently, she had attempted to get up and had fallen hitting her head on the marble mantlepiece in her bedroom.

Some weeks later Mrs Ogilvie Smyth's last will and testament was read with only two beneficiaries. Good hearted Sadie McIntosh was named chief beneficiary, and a very small bequest for Jodie Crichton.

The solicitor, Mr Dingwall, peered at Jodie over his horn-rimmed spectacles.

> 'The first named beneficiary Ms Sadie McIntosh unfortunately expired prior to the passing of Mrs Ogilvy-Smyth, so in this case Mrs Ogilvy-Smyth's whole estate will now pass to you Miss Jodie Crichton. We can help you with investments. You are now an exceptionally wealthy young woman.'

The Pick Up

Yummy mummies, Molly and Fay, joked and chatted animatedly over a cuppa, as they dreamt up notions of leading more fulfilling lives.

Both were doting mothers and loving wives - but how wonderful would it be to hold down a high-flying job too? Perhaps as buyer for C & A or Area Manager for Wallis. Maybe fly down to London or Paris on a day trip, to attend fashion shows and exhibitions. They could hob nob with top designers and meet famous celebrities. They contemplated that everybody would listen with fascination to **their** innovative ideas. To attain the glory of accomplishment and, other than motherhood, be acclaimed and appreciated by peers. That was their goal.

Then, after a busy day at 'work' each day, they'd return home for five o'clock to cook fish fingers and beans for the bairns' suppers. Once the weans were bathed and bedded, the fashionistas would cuddle up with respective hubbies, to exchange exciting stories of the day, over a cocoa.

It was a pipe dream!

Brainstorming was a regular pastime for the girls; in search for inspiration and entertain themselves with an endless list of career prospects.

Then one day, Fay's husband offered a surprise proposal - a part-time sales role with his car radiator company, which they could job-share; only two mornings each, per week.

'You'll be cracking, it'll be great fun and the customers will love you,' Ben assured them. 'All you have to do is drive the company van to visit our regular contacts. You'll pick up leaky radiators then deliver the repaired goods back to customers the following day. *Easy peasy*. Banter with the guys; a wee smile; make their day.'

Fay was, of-course, mega enthusiastic. However, with zero knowledge or interest in motor parts, Molly wished with all her heart the product was *haute couture* designer handbags. But she conceded it might be good sales experience.

So, 1980s fashion dolly Molly, with feathered haircut, 'power' dressed for her new sales driver role; in a pink Dash top and figure hugging Levis which were neatly tucked into tan suede pixie boots from which tassles freely dangled. Lippy applied, then a quick check that her oversized *Sue Ellen Ewing* shoulder pads were straight, she was ready to face her new challenge.

First day at work is always nerve wrecking, but she had listened carefully to Ben's instructions, trying to memorise her introduction spiel and the names of all the storemen on her sales visit round.

'Oor Fred's in a union meeting wi' the bosses. Just wait and he'll be back in a jiff,' the garage mechanic, at the Union Glen Ford's garage, advised.

A posse of around fifty workshop fitters and mechanics had gathered in the storeroom awaiting their shop steward. Molly suddenly felt out of place and flustered as she sensed peering eyes which were blatantly checking out the new girl on the block. Radio One was playing through the workshop speakers and a few of the guys sang along to *Reet Petite,* '….lookabel, lookabel Oooooh Weeeeee …' She resisted the urge to join in (and boogee). She didn't dare. Tapping her pointy ankle boot impatiently…… she smiled. The wait was only a few minutes but felt like hours.

'I'm no bimbo, they'll soon see!' she mused.

At snail-pace, bespectacled storeman Fred, in his long blue overall, finally appeared.

'Hi Fred, I'm Molly from Bon Accord Radiators,' she announced chirpily, 'I'm here to collect a radiator for repair.'

Apparently in a crabby mood after a disagreeable outcome at the Union meeting, Fred grunted and brusquely pointed in the direction of a bundle of car parts sitting in the corner. Without dilly-dally, and in haste to escape the crazy place, she scanned her eyes towards the pile then reaching out, she scooped the nearest hefty item up in her arms. Struggling to carry it but determined to show herself as capable, and not at all ditzy, she trotted through the workshop towards the company white Ford transit van which she had parked outside.

By now Billy Joel's vocals, of *Uptown Girl*, were blaring amidst a chorus of catcalls and wolf-whistles which grew louder and louder and LOUDER.

'Oh God,' she thought, flustered with embarrassment, *'**Please**, get me out of here.'*

Christie Brinkley need have no worries of dance move competition as Molly's Kurt Geiger boots picked up speed and she waddled as fast as she could muster. While bursting the rear doors open to load the heavy item into the van, a strong hairy hand suddenly grabbed her shoulder. She shrieked.

'Sunshine,' the hunky mechanic ridiculed, 'THAT's not a radiator, THAT's a bumper!'

BRIDGES TRILOGY

A Very Posh Council Estate
A Hollywood Smile
Homecoming

also
Guerra Civil Española

A Very Posh Council Estate

In the 50s, 60s and 70s, Ashgrove was considered THE 'posh' council estate in Aberdeen and some of its proud residents classed themselves as *a cut above*!

Post WW2, housing conditions across Britain were derelict, dilapidated and ruinously run-down. Aberdeen was no different. Most tenement buildings still had outside shared 'lavvies' with cut-out squares of newspaper hanging on a string – **not** for reading by the way. Andrex was unaffordable. A chamberpot, or chuntie, would be kept under the bed in case of emergency during the night The tin bath would come out for the family's weekly wash and filled with hot bathwater which was heated on a hanging kettle over the open fire, to be reused by priority status – eldest child first, youngest last.

Sunday bath-time would be concluded with a spoonful of castor oil; ensuring both clean exterior AND cleansed interior! A morning shave and after work wash was conducted at the kitchen sink.

Each flat was assigned a 'day of the week' for use of the rat infested wash-house in the basement, drying attic and washing green. Women (alias unpaid skivvies) of the house would struggle carting heavy baskets of washing and kettles of water up and down the back stairs. They'd scrub the weekly laundry on a washboard using carbolic soap or Lux soap flakes, then hand rinse out every sud of soapy lather before wringing the soaking wet sheets, towels, clothes and underwear through the mangle. Manically turning the hand wheel round and round, their hands were red and swollen and sweat dripped from their brows. It was heavy work. Weather permitting, the washing would be hung out on the back-green (or backie) wash line and propped up by a long wooden pole. Shirts, semmits, long drawers and combinations would dance freely and in abundance, up high in the North East breeze.

Vermin was rife. Living conditions were damp and cramped. The pungent smell of moth balls lingered on linen and clothes, but it was unavoidable. With little option of accommodation, newlyweds usually had to squeeze in with parents and siblings, thus resulting in further stress to a household, already 'burstin' at the seams. Sometimes, if possible, young couples would find an empty old army hut on a deserted army camp to squat in and this was a better alternative to the daily squabbling back home.

In the fifties, US designed pre-fab self-contained houses were hastily constructed en masse, much to the delight of their lucky new tenants. Although these were 'temporary' construction homes with an initial shelf life of around twenty years, they were considered luxurious; self-contained bungalows with own garden.

Aberdeen City Council created new housing schemes which popped up here, there and everywhere; but, sadly, not fast enough! New modern homes were still in very short supply. Young couples with families were **desperate** to secure a trendy council house.

It seemed like eternity for young couple Annie and Jimmy as they endured a three year wait for an offer.

Their attic flat in East North Street had two rooms; a living room and a bedroom. With no running water, even with a young baby, Annie had to regularly negotiate rickety wooden steps, to and from the top floor and basement, to collect kettles and pales of water. They kept a one-eyed tiger cat called Meenie who was no sweet, loving pussy; she was a working pet – a ratter. Jimmy would fetch the coal and sticks daily from the cellar in the back garden, to light the fire in the black cast iron range which not only provided heat for the poky flat but fired up the oven and stove. The water kettle hung permanently atop the fire. All daily activities, including cooking and bathing, took place in the paltry living room. And of-course the lavvie was shared by **six** households.

United in their protest against the Victorian-like living conditions, all tenants in the building demanded Council housing and, ultimately, they all withheld their rent from their private landlord. When the landlord's prosecution case came to court, the judge forgave the unpaid rent and decreed Annie and Jimmy and all their neighbours would no longer have to pay. But this did not help their plight as they were yearning to move from the hell hole.

So, that Spring day in 1957 when the Bridges family moved into the middle floor flat, 30 Gillespie Crescent, with their young daughter, an elated Annie felt like she'd won jackpot at the Bingo.

The Ashgrove scheme was enclosed by an eight-foot high drystone wall which was bordered by stunning, tall, historic Ash trees. A spacious well-kept grass park sat at the grand entrance and on one side of the sweeping crescent sat a row of cute OAP terraced cottages, each with a small, colourful rockery front garden.

No 1 Gillespie Crescent, the prime corner cottage adjacent to the park, was occupied by *Labour Councillor Robert Lennox* and as time went on, when he was appointed *Lord Provos*t, a luxurious shiny ebony black, Rolls Royce parked outside his garden. Proudly adorning the Bon Accord crest flag on it's bonnet and the Aberdeen City Council coat of arms emblazoned on the doors, the majestic vehicle and Mr Lennox's presence in Ashgrove, served to further raise the profile of the scheme. For those living nearby, it was akin to living next door to Royalty. When making polite exchange about the weather to Lord Provost Lennox, the Aberdonian dialect of 'wifie' neighbours, would miraculously transform to high pitched *faux posh*!

Springtime, Gillespie Crescent's sweeping pavements were lined with dozens of glorious cherry blossom trees, all bearing sweet scented pink floral blooms. The scheme predominantly consisted of six flatted modern tenements. Each flat comprised a lounge, two bedrooms, kitchen, bathroom, hot water tank cupboard, own coal cellar and a veranda. In the centre of the lounge sat a small modern Art Deco tiled fireplace.

A plot of garden was allotted to each tenant and residents took great pride in their homes, gardens and environment. All front gardens were allotted to ground floor tenants who manicured them lovingly, always mindful of competition from their neighbours. It was not unusual to see Sunday strollers admiring the plethora of garden flowers, bushes, small trees and … comical garden gnomes.

This conscientious pride in the environment extended to the buildings' common stairs too where a cleaning rota was adhered to religiously and any housewife tenant who ignored it, did so at their peril. No self-respecting 'wifie' would dare be the topic of the neighbours' vicious gossip - nor risk losing their tenancy.

A year after moving in, a letter arrived at No 30, addressed to Jimmy. The envelope was stamped *Aberdeen City Council.* He ripped it open, unaware of its contents. It advised …

> ' … *a neighbour complaint has been raised about your unkempt plot of ground. You are advised that, within the terms of your tenancy, you must maintain your garden to an acceptable standard within four weeks otherwise your Council Tenancy Agreement may be terminated…*'

The clock was ticking….

Jimmy's face was ashen with shock. He was born and bred in Edinburgh, in an overcrowded top floor flat of a sandstone tenement in the impoverished Port of Leith. With absolutely zero 'horticultural' knowledge, he was clueless as to how to design, plant or maintain a garden. Working ten to twelve hour shifts, five or six days a week, driving his 'rock 'n roll' Scania Scarab lorry, left him with neither energy nor motivation to dig up his hilly slope plot, which was now piled high in weeds. But this letter was matter-of-fact – **fix it or flit out**!

The clock was ticking…

An unholy war ensued. When Annie read the ominous threat, to lose her dream home, she panicked. She freaked out. *She lost the heid!* Her wrath was not only aimed at Jimmy but spilled over to the neighbours too as like Miss Marple, she was on a mission to find out the name of the poison pen writer.

The clock was ticking…

In desperation, for green finger advice, Jimmy asked around his crony workmates who hung out at his workingman's pub, the Lorne Bar. How could he fix the garden – **in a hurry**? After lively, boozy garden-related tips and suggestions, the discussion grew noisier with each round of drinks. Jimmy's dilemma was 'lost in translation.'

The following evening when he staggered home from a hard day's graft and a few pints in his belly, he was met with an enraged, seething Annie.

Cursing in her curlers, she pointed towards her lounge window.

'Fit the f***ing hell is THAT oan oor f***ing gairden?'

That day, a ton of *dung* was delivered and tipped on their plot by a well-wishing pal. It was steaming and it **stank**!

With the clock still ticking…

Nosy neighbours peeked behind their net curtains while a dispirited Jimmy spent the next few weekends, with spade in hand digging the abundance of fertiliser into the soil. He planted spuds which, he was promised, would prepare the earth well for sowing grass seed.

Annie and Jimmy were not on speaking terms for the duration of the garden rescue and the atmosphere in No 30 resembled *that* manure.

In time, *Lord Provost Robert Lennox* would be regularly visited by his pretty young, blonde, blue eyed and musical niece Anne who would befriend the little girl in No 30. *Who's that girl?*

A Hollywood Smile

*P*ost *WW2 in Britain, in the newly founded NHS, extraction of ALL teeth with replacement of full upper and lower dentures became widespread. For dentists in both the NHS and private sector, this was a viable solution for patients with poor dental health and few existing teeth. And it was also financially lucrative for the dental practitioners. However, by the 70s, there were many cases where women, in particular, with perfectly healthy nashers, hankered after 'A Hollywood Smile' – and they'd take this drastic cosmetic action – which was* NHS FREE.

Annie's story

A factory 'girl' all my life in Aberdeen, I was working at Lawsons of Dyce on the night shift 10pm 'til 7am on a 40 hours week. My highly paid weekly wage compensated for the unsociable working hours and chill temperature working environment in the meat processing plant.

Each evening, after arriving at work by car share, we'd head to the changing room to stash our stuff in our lockers. The workforce would don the unbecoming white uniforms, tucking every strand of hair under the netting of white peaked hats and pull on a pair of white welly boots. Underneath the long, baggy overalls we wore warm woolly jumpers and cosy tights. Even a hint of pink lipstick could not detract from our cold red noses and the hideous, unsexy attire. We'd emerge to start our shift on the factory floor like an army of Tetley tea folk.

I'd pack bacon and gammon on the Marks and Spencer line as the Berkel slicer chugged back and forth, back and forth, all night long; keeping time with the seconds on the clock; back and forth, tick tock. Monotonous. The drone of the fridges and slicing machines would be drowned out, in part, by the non-stop chatter and gossip of the lassies. Just about stuff. Anything and everything. Sometimes of importance and sometimes a load of tosh. Sharing experiences, good and bad, funny or sad. It killed the boredom of the tedious repetitive production line whilst keeping us awake in the early hours of the morning. We'd joke, we'd banter, we'd gossip, we'd take the piss out of upstart young male supervisors.

'Where's Madge? Tea-break finished ten minutes ago,' wee Mikey once naively demanded authoritatively.

'She's looking for a tampax! Do you have any?' Ada joked.

The girls nudged each other with glee while observing the loon's face reddening and squirming in discomfort.

The lads soon caught on that to keep schtum and ask no questions, was preferable to the banter we'd bat back. Oh, how we'd laugh!

And ANY newbies to the team who displayed airs and graces and stepped out of line would be sharply shot down. That was the way.

But we were a loyal bunch and showed camaraderie and empathy to each other. If one of us experienced a personal problem, we'd rally round to help if we could, even if it was just well-meaning advice or a trusting ear to listen. And many a drama update was whispered down the production line – Maisie's cheating partner; Jean's brow beaten jailed sister who murdered her drunken lout of a husband; the infamous tantrum Babs threw when humiliated by Hughie Green on an audition for Opportunity Knocks.

Apart from the notice board in the canteen, there was always tittle tattle update on any Trade Union (TUC) meetings which the day shift shop steward attended. The girls on night shift were not particularly interested in union discussion – however, if the topic related to their wage packet or working hours THEN they we were all ears. When the shop steward called 'everybody out,' the night shift staff, in general, were not in agreement to strike – unless there was an fluke summer heatwave. A day or two off work to sun themselves was always very welcome! But with nightshift bonus, the money was good, conditions satisfactory and the girls could little afford disruption to their incomes.

Like Facebook today, we also shared invaluable tips; how to get elusive Tivoli tickets to see Frankie Vaughan or seats for Francie and Josie at the glorious

Her Majesty's Theatre; recommendation on cheap carpet shops; how to get through the menopause or cures for a migraine. Above all, we listened, to workmates' dilemmas, always with a sympathetic ear. This was networking and counselling 70s style.

When thirty-four year old colleague, mother of two, Sheena had all her teeth pulled and replaced with beautiful straight pure white false teeth, the shop floor was buzzing. It was not that dentures were a *nouveau* invention, but they were never before fitted **purely** for cosmetic purposes. We listened intently to her step by step account. Like a group of nosey chimps, we piled around to examine her brand new, pearly whites and interrogated the brave soul. How sore was it? How long did it take? Which dentist she attended?

'It wisnae too bad and ma dentist Mr Duff was so kind. I really liked him. And he's dishy, looks like Omar Sharif,' she swooned. 'It took aboot an hour then I went hame and ma man heated a tin o' Baxters soup for me an' the kids. Last week, I took a sickie from work but yesterday I got my new teeth fitted. My gums are still a wee bit tender but I feel like I've got a new lease of life.'

Her new 'glamourous' look was indeed effective even in her grossly unattractive Lawson's overalls.

So, one day after an excruciating, painful filling at the dentist, with the screeching, high-pitched, grinding sound of the drill which caused unexpected shooting pain down an unsuspecting nerve, I decided, 'NEVER AGAIN.' Six months later I made an appointment with Mr Duff.

'Next Tuesday, ah'm gan tae get a' ma teeth oot. Ah'll be under anaesthetic so will you come wi' me?' I asked my daughter Bridget.

'Are you aff yer heid?' she retorted in shock, spilling her tea in the process. 'To get them ALL out is DRASTIC. Totally unnecessary. Nothing wrong with your teeth. You're still young.'

But I was adamant. I'd looked, I'd listened and I'd liked. It's what **I** wanted.

So, Tuesday morning October 2nd, 1973 we precariously entered the packed but pin-drop quiet dentist waiting room. Tuesday was *'Extraction'* day.

We couldn't find a seat together so I squeezed my shapely bum between two very unhappy men, both obviously grisly in pain, each holding their hands to swollen faces; me, on one side of the room and Bridget perkily sitting on the other.

Nerves are a weird phenomenon. They can make you cry with fear, shiver and shake in anticipation of the unknown, or even poop yourself. But worse still, as in our case, quite cruelly bring on inappropriate behaviour - with a fit of the giggles. It didn't usually take much to set us off. Today, it was the glum faces of the poor, suffering patients around us, all awaiting dental doom in deathly silence. Not a word or sound in the room except for an occasional moan and groan, sometimes even a wee squeal would escape a hurting gob. Bridget avoided eye contact with me but I could see her shoulders jittering – then we were off!

We stifled our laughter until we could hold it no more. Tears rolled down our cheeks. We were so embarrassed in the otherwise silent room, but helpless to stop. I knew the pain of these poor souls would soon be my own fate but that just seemed more comical. Why? I really don't know.

'Annie Bridges,' the dental assistant called.

Well, THAT wiped the smile from my face. With trepidation in a jolt of intense fear, I was led by the arm to the dentist chair as if facing execution.

'Annie, please start counting,' came the instruction from '*Omar Sharif.*' 'One, two, three….' My arms and legs writhed and thrashed as the grewsome big black rubber mask was plonked on my face - then claustrophobia triggered terror, like never before.

An hour later, I was still in the recovery room and the dental assistant was patting my face and wiping my mouth with blood-stained tissues while calling my name to bring me round. The pungent smell and taste of general anaesthesia lingered as I groaned over a sick bowl. Bridget asked reception to call for a taxi and I was given an appointment to come back the following week for denture fitment.

With the familiar whiff of McEwans beer on his breath, my Jimmy came home for his tea, just after six. His mince and tatties were blissfully ready. As usual, he headed to the kitchen where he discarded his bunnet, damp jacket and oily dungarees then, sitting on a stool, he unlaced and kicked off one black leather steel-toed boot – THUD, then the other – THUD.

Neighbour Zena downstairs was used to this familiar din which signalled the man in No 30 was home!

His face was a picture of horror when he saw me wi' nae teeth and he roared as his stool gave way beneath him. He assumed I'd been in an accident. It was a shock for him. He didnae ken. I didnae tell him. He went mad when I *telt* him. But I was creative with the truth and with a crocodile tear and a toothless lisp, I wept as I told him that the dentist recommended it 'cos he diagnosed diarrhoea. I meant to say *piorrea*.

'It'll all be worth it when he sees my beautiful new teeth,' I thought, '… and, never again anither visit tae the dentist.'

With tender, sore gums and a low pain threshold, I dreaded the return visit. Contemplating the pain of something or somebody touching my oral wounds, essential of-course for fitting new dentures, was unbearable. But the following Wednesday afternoon as planned, I sauntered down to the Belmont Road surgery.

'What's this?' I puzzled when I found the surgery's front door locked with a sign.

To all patients.
We regret to advise that this dental surgery is closed
until further notice.

M Duff

My first reaction was a sense of relief. 'No pain today, the dentist's gone away…' But curiosity sent me to the Vet next door, just to inquire.

'Mr Duff's done a runner. Disappeared. No one knows where he is,' the receptionist relayed with great zeal '…but his wife is on the warpath. He's left her with three kids and a string of debt. Not a word of warning. Gone off with a floozy we think …'

Now this **was** a piece of juicy gossip. The Lawsons girls would relish it when I returned to work that night without new dentures and a face like a squashed purse. And, of-course, they did. Sheena said she couldn't believe it, especially about the debts.

I took a lot of jibes and jokes at work as I was nicknamed '*cabbage patch doll*,' and god knows what else behind my back. I just rose above it. I kind of seen the funny side. Sheena was so supportive, offering a kindly ear and I returned the compassion as I heard of the domestic rift at home with her jealous husband.

The b**tard threw her out and she was fighting to see her kids. So heart-breaking. It took my mind off my own predicament.

Next day, I decided to give myself a copper wash-in rinse to my mousey brown hair. It would surely cheer me up. It was the first time I'd tried it but I'd heard the Lawsons lassies talking. After washing my hair, I applied the sachet then wrapped a towel around my head while I cleaned the house in preparation for the weekend. It was supposed to be rinsed off after 5-10 minutes but I thought, '*What the hell!*' I continued dusting, hoovering, laundry, mopping and outside cleaning. It was around two hours later that I washed the colour out, put my curlers in and afterwards it was off to bed for much needed sleep prior to the night shift.

The following day, Bridget was ready and dressed with tartan trolley in hand, waiting to go with me for food shopping to Berryden Norco. She screamed hysterically.

'What's wrong? Stop being melodramatic!' I demanded.

'Your hair's CRIMSON! What have you done?'

At the dressing table mirror, I studied my coloured barnet more closely and felt a bit woozy and sick. As if a gurning face was not bad enough, I now had crazy red hair.

'What'll I do?' I panicked. 'But it's only a rinse and supposed to wash out by 4 weeks. I'll just give it a good shampoo. It'll be OK,' I surmised.

I shampooed it with Vosene, then Fairy Liquid, then, in desperation, I scrubbed it with handfuls of Arial washing powder, washing and rinsing it again and again – until it turned iridescent shocking pink. You learn something every day. Who would have thought? The more you wash tinted rinse hair, the brighter the hues become. From the mirror reflection, all I could see was a *punk*.

Over that weekend, unexpectedly and very sadly, a telegram arrived to advise that a relative of Jimmy's in Edinburgh had tragically died. Of-course we'd have to attend the funeral. The drama of my dental disaster temporarily faded with the sadness. I donned a hat for the car journey hoping my strange hairdo would be hidden from sour faced Jimmy and his Edine folks.

The funeral party walked past me in non-recognition of my 'collapsed' face, whilst also trying to ignore the candy floss peeking out from under my black furry hat. It was just SO hard. My speech was severely distorted. Trying to offer my sincere condolences and explain my plight with 'nae teeth' and a punk-like hairdo was a challenge, especially when naebody could understand a word. Again, there is a fine line between intense sadness and the urge to go apeshit with laughter. It was *really* tough.

One week passed, then another, then another. I didn't worry too much at first but when my gums healed and didn't hurt any more, and with Jimmy's daily nagging, I decided it was time to ask another dentist surgery to fit my false teeth.

Disbelief. Incredulity.

> *'Mrs Bridges, it is a contract between the NHS and the dental practitioner for the undertaking of teeth extraction and replacement denture fitment. Unfortunately, no dentist neither NHS nor private, can carry out work on a patient during their treatment unless that original contractual dental practitioner agrees to nullify the contract.'*

'So dis that mean I huv tae wait for AWOL Duff tae come back?'

'Exactly' was the reply.

Toothless and gummy is not a good look, especially when you are only in your forties, but what could I do? I must wait. Patience has never been a virtue of mine. **Now** this was definitely **not** funny. I rued the day I took this stupid, daft decision. What an eejit I'd been. And Jimmy harped on about it on a daily basis. He was affronted of me.

As Xmas and New Year festivities drew nearer, I felt a cloud of depression hovering over me. Three months had passed and still no word of the nomad dentist who left me in limbo. Obsessed with the pickle I was in, it was on my mind 24/7 and I couldn't escape the worry. The prospect of never, ever again having teeth seemed to become a sad reality. Weeping myself to sleep each night, I hated and cursed Duff with a vengeance. Had it not been for his disappearance, I'd have now been sporting 'A Hollywood Smile' and not felt like an oddity. Partying to *Chirpy Chirpy Cheap Cheap* like a toothless wonder was not in my festive plans.

Bridget ordered me to *pull myself together*.

'Just get dolled up, put on your glad rags and a bit of make up and *pretend* your teeth are still there.'

We were all ready to first foot our neighbours, to bring in the New Year 1974 bells, the first of many house parties. But when Bridget came back home, after being out with her friends, she clocked my muppet face wearing bright hot-red lipstick and my new tight curl home perm, still pink-tinged. She collapsed in a heap with laughter. It's not that she's unkind; she just couldn't help herself.

At Lawsons, the girls were so sympathetic and the whereabouts of b**tard Duff were always the hot topic of discussion. Imaginative hunches as to his disappearance were creatively suggested; he fled to Australia; he put a floozy *up the spout*; he changed his name and opened another practice down south. Another theory flailed that he'd been involved in a horrific accident and may be suffering from amnesia! Much as I hoped the latter to be true and visualised him lying, suffering in a gutter somewhere, of-course I didn't want this, because I was willing my nightmare to end. I just needed him FOUND!

Two months later, good news came in the shape of a letter from Grampian Health Board HQ. It indicated the dental wanderer had returned and this was an invitation for me to attend his malpractice tribunal, set for 10am Wednesday 3rd April, 1974. The notification also conveyed that refusal to attend or give evidence, would delay my treatment **indefinitely.**

So, on that sunny Spring morning, just over six months after Duff's '*Extraction' Tuesday*,' I registered my attendance at his tribunal. The traditional silver granite building in Aberdeen's West End, 42 Queen's Road was very grand with high ceiling period features and a plush red carpet. All of a sudden, I was again overcome with a waft of inferiority and unworthiness. But pangs of guilt hit hard, that the words of a Lawsons cold meat packer could strike off a man's glowing career. I wanted to run.

The efficacious receptionist directed me to the waiting room. Slowly pushing the creaky, heavy, oak door open, there before me was a sight to behold.

A dozen or so toothless souls, some I recognised from '*Extraction' Tuesday*' - ALL there, present and correct, to give evidence. A room full of 'muppets,' 'cabbage patch dolls' and 'gurners'. I felt at last I belonged. Not ONE tooth between us. I howled with laughter … and they joined in. Hilarity soared from the normally sombre stately room!

But in the corner, I spied the inconspicuous presence of someone I knew.

'Hello, Sheena?' I yelled as I darted over to sit beside her.

'Fit ye daein' here?'

Her whispered response floored me.

'I'm here to give evidence in support of Murdo.'

Bewildered and befuddled, the *F* word fumbled around on my pursed lips, *'F..F..F.. F***ing Floozy!'*

Homecoming

January 1976

Bridget's reflection mirrored from the grubby train window as she rested her forehead pensively against the cold clammy glass in the draughty compartment. The overnight train, KingsX-Aberdeen was approaching Montrose.

With a loud bang from the heavy compartment door as it slammed open, a cheery British Rail uniformed ticket inspector hollered 'Tickets!'

It tickled Bridget to hear the Aberdonian twang again. OH, how she'd missed hearing it for the last two years.

A bleary-eyed young man sprawled out on the well-worn upholstered seat opposite her woke up with a start, slaver dripping from his chin which he sheepishly wiped away. His embarrassment would have been tenfold had he heard his intermittent hog-like snoring and snorting which lasted for a couple of hours during his travel slumber.

Only one hour to go. Home soon. Her heart skipped a beat.

One day previous, she boarded the British Airways BA301 flight Istanbul to London Heathrow with a tear stained face after kissing her beloved fiancé goodbye. The notion of being apart was tortuous, but a necessary torment. Six months of long-distance planning, whilst basking bikini clad in the Antalya burning sun, the tan blonde was now finally back in cold drizzly Scotland to finalise the details for her big day – her Wedding Day. Her heart skipped a beat.

In those *soleil* daydreams, she pictured her homecoming and the happy faces of her ma 'n da, Annie and Jimmy, so eager to see their only child again. They must've missed her so much, she reflected. They would be waiting for her on Platform One with Bridget's precious pooch, Schmooky.

Schmooky was a miniature blue and tan Yorkshire Terrier, or at least that's what his Kennel Club pedigree certificate indicated. A cute fluffy mutt for her to groom and dress with a ribbon in his hair. Like many things in her life, Bridget's plans often went awry; she often tried to shake off that minxy jinx that was permanently perched on her shoulder.

An only child is a lonely child and Bridget had craved for a dog all her childhood – a wee pal to cuddle and care for and keep her company. As a youngster, she would regularly knock on neighbours' doors.

'Can I take your dog for a walk?'

Invariably the reply was 'Aye, tak her tae the shops and get me a ten o' Woodbine.'

Sometimes the shopping list included golden tan seamed stockings or a can of Silvikrin hair spray. But Bridget didn't mind, she just loved walking dogs on a lead, chatting to them on her stroll, pretending they were human chums.

As her 21st birthday approached, while living and working around Heathrow Airport, she pleaded with the love of her life, Zafer, to buy her a puppy. He was definitely not keen. From early childhood, he developed a fear of dogs initiated by a scary dog bite and the painful rabies injections that followed. But sympathetic to her longing, he reluctantly conceded. Bridget contemplated that a small dog would be less threatening for him and so phoned Chalfont St Giles Kennels to enquire in her thick Aberdonian accent if they had small pups. The breeder responded in a thick Cockney accent, *'Yes, a miniature Yorkshire Terrier is available.'*

On arrival at the farm, the breeder led them to a cow shed where a straw lined tea box sat in the corner with four adorable pups, all differing breeds, wriggling and squealing around in the hay.

'That's a miniature Yorkie there,' she pointed out.

It was love at first sight. The minute Bridget set eyes on the tiny quivering and shivering ball of fluff, her heart melted and Zafer duly parted with £50, equating to a couple of weeks wages. Bridget noted from Schmooky's Kennel Club Pedigree Certificate that the pup was only five weeks old but as a novice dog owner, she accepted the breeder's advice that he was *'good to go'*.

That night, in bed, Schmooky snuggled up in the nape of Bridget's neck. The tiny pup adamantly rejected the comfy wee dog basket which was awaiting his arrival. After a sleepless night, he was offered breakfast of Farley's rusk mashed with milk but Bridget noticed her tiny pet's uncontrollable scratching so she prepared a warm bath for him with Johnson's baby shampoo in her bathroom sink. It left him sleepy so she gently laid him in his little bed. After a couple of hours, she bent down to pick him up. To her absolute horror and disgust, he was covered in dandruff – white dandruff - which moved! It was lice.

'*AAGH AAGH AAGH*!'

The heat had evidently hatched nits' eggs. Picking the wee mite up in a towel, she rushed him to a vet practice where she was given medicated shampoo and a nit comb. But that emergency visit sadly revealed in vet examination that from the patchy hair loss on Schmooky's body, he may be suffering from a hormone imbalance which would likely result in Alopecia. Although his tan hair may grow, it was probable that he would be destined for a life of blue hair baldness. On the vet's instructions, she contacted the kennels, the belligerent breeder was matter of fact, without empathy or apology, offering a refund if she returned *'the little runt'*.

'**What**?' Bridget exclaimed, '… **return** Schmooky? And **what** *Runt*? How very dare she?'

Of-course returning her 'adorable' pup was out of the question as within a mere 24 hours, the bond meant she could NEVER part with him. After about a week or so, apart from his tan hairy paws and a fluffy tan mane framing his cheeky wee face, he was blue skin and bone. Bald as a newt. Not a pretty sight.

And so, it came to pass, this weird looking little dog would fit right in with her dysfunctional family. Subsequently, for the past two years while she was living in Turkey, he lived with Annie and Jimmy.

As the train stopped briefly at Stonehaven, Bridget's recollection abruptly ceased. Only thirty minutes from home. Not long now. Her heart skipped a beat.

She suddenly recalled the news from her mum's last letter. Dad had lost his driving licence for nine months *'for being in charge of a vehicle while under the influence of alcohol'*. It transpired that, feeling the worse for wear after a pint or two after work, he parked his Ford

Anglia, to take a nap – and subsequently he was found fast asleep at the wheel, *outside Lodge Walk Police Station*. What a numpty!

The repercussions could have been long lasting since Jimmy was a British Rail HGV lorry driver. But because of his glowing work record for attendance and safety, his boss generously did not fire him. He was, instead, demoted to yard labourer for the duration of the licence ban. Duties included cleaning up after his snidy, gloating workmates in the bothy; making the tea and washing their mugs. With the bump down from Senior Driver, his pride took a hit and his mood was black. 'Who would suffer most?' Bridget reflected. 'Jimmy? His sarky workmates? Or wife Annie?'

Bridget hoped her ma 'n da would set aside the squabbling, scrapping, screaming, sulking and dramas she remembered so well from childhood. Set it all aside for this happy event. She felt sure they would. Her heart skipped a beat.

Speeding past Portlethen, her destination station was looming. So much to organise in the next three months. Invitations; venue; menus; flowers; cake;

cars; dinner suits for the groom, the best man and the father of the bride. It was a shame her beloved would not agree to wear a traditional dress kilt for their nuptials. She'd love to see him in beautiful tartan but she conceded that her dad Jimmy would also kick up a stink if forced to wear a kilt and reveal his chicken-skinny legs.

First priority, to find that fairy-tale wedding dress. Where to shop? What style - puffball or fitted? White or perhaps cream? Train or no train? Long veil, short veil or hat?

Bridget had relented that a Wedding March down the aisle was disappointingly out of the question since Zafer had firmly refused to marry in church. He looked at her in disbelief when she suggested they could have TWO ceremonies – one in a mosque in Istanbul and one in Aberdeen's St Machar's Cathedral.

'In Turkey, we do not get married in mosques. The Imam does not carry out a wedding ceremony,' he pointed out, '…unless you want me to take many more wives!'

So, Aberdeen Registrar it must be …

With the Bay of Nigg in view, the silver sands of Aberdeen gradually appeared in the distance. Then the familiar sight of oil rigs, tankers and fishing trawlers which dotted the vast expanse of the grey, choppy North Sea.

The train was now steadily approaching Aberdeen station. The guard's whistle blew. The essence of steam, diesel, oil and rail track wafted as the lazy clunking train wheels laboured and chugged to a halt. All of a sudden, there was a buzzing rush of fellow passengers lifting their heavy luggage from the overhead racks whilst creating congestion as they squeezed past each other in the corridor. As soon as the train doors banged open, the impatient passengers started to disembark in a very disorderly fashion, on to the platform below. Bridget waited in the compartment for the bustle to pass.

She had arrived. She took a deep breath. Her heart skipped a beat.

Guerra Civil Española

Edinburgh, January 1937

No cheers, no jeers, no smiles, no tears.

Throngs of indifferent onlookers lined Leith Walk. Curious wifies hung out of their tenement windows. The VX International Brigadiers; proud husbands, fathers and sons, swiftly advanced in dignified fashion, with camaraderie and supporters towards Edinburgh Waverley Station.

No uniforms, no glory, no regiment, no military band; only civvy clothes and stalwart comradeship behind the *'Solidarity for Spain'* banner.

Clutching his pregnant mother's hand, a six year old laddie in the crowd waved goodbye to his daddy.

Eight decades later, Jimmy raises a wee dram to Robert Bridges, who fought and fell at Jarama. He sadly reminisces that last farewell — and reflects what might have been...

Granny's in the Kitchen

A 1950s children's story

Mo clasped her small chubby hands together in front of her older sister in a begging gesture.

'Can I have a shot? Awe, please Trisha. Teach me how to skip…Pleeese.'

'Go away Mo, go and play with your own friends,' Trisha frowned.

'I'm going to tell Mum you wouldn't let me play with you again.' The little girl stamped her foot.

'Your wee sister's a serious pest isn't she,' Trisha's friend Fiona tutted.

The other two girls cawed the long length of rope, stretching their arms out in wide circular arching movements. Each time the rope scuffed the ground, a wiry curly-headed girl in the middle of the game hop-stepped over it in quick light movements, her fists clenched at her sides as she concentrated on keeping the rhythm to the song,

> *'Granny's in the kitchen doing some stitching.*
> *In comes a bogie man and chases granny out.'*

This was the moment in the game where she had to skip out from the cawing rope and the next girl skipped in.

> *'Granny's in the kitchen doing some stitching....'*

'Ah go on Trisha. Give me a shottie...' Mo persisted. 'When can I have a turn?' she whined determinedly, pushing in front of her big sister who was next in the queue.

'Yer a right wee scunner. You need a good skelp!' Trisha gripped her little sister from behind and digging her fingers into her bony shoulders pushed her aside.

'Awe Trisha.'

Trisha's friend Fiona gave a long, exaggerated sigh.

'Just let her have a wee shot.'

She turned to Mo with her hand on her hip.

'Then will you promise to go away and leave us in peace?' Mo nodded her head vigorously giving Fiona a wide, gap-toothed smile.

Trisha flicked her pigtail and shrugged.

'I suppose you can have just one shot Mo but you'll have to put your dolly down. You can't learn to skip holding a dolly at the same time.'

Mo shook her head.

'I won't put Hetty down Trisha,' she lisped petulantly. 'She's my friend. She can skip with me.'

Trisha rolled her eyes and stepping back she shoved Mo forward muttering in an exasperated tone.

'You're such a spoiled brat Mo. On you go then.'

The girls halted cawing the rope to allow Mo to run into the middle. She stood motionless clutching her dolly, waiting.

'OK, get ready to jump Mo.' The girls began to caw the rope slowly. Mo easily jumped over each turn.'

'Fathter.' she lisped.

'You want us to caw faster? Do you want to learn how to do the bumps Mo?' One of the girls asked in a lilting northern accent.

'*Yeah, I want to do the bumps.*' Mo mimicked the girl's accent, annoyingly showing off now.

The girls began to caw harder and faster. Mo had to jump higher and faster to miss the whipping rope as it circled round and round.

Her feet began to drag. At the next turn of the rope she failed to lift them high enough and the rope tangled round her ankle tripping her up. With a horrible jolt, Mo felt herself tumble forward and throwing her arms out to save herself she let go of her doll. She could only watch helpless as it sailed out of her arms, its head hitting the cobble stones and breaking. Sprawled on the ground on all fours Mo felt a sharp pain in her knee. A huge cry welled up inside her then she bawled blue murder. Trisha and Fiona quickly hauled the youngster to her feet.

'Awe, stop yer howlin' Mo.' Trisha felt embarrassed by her wee sister's raucous wailing. 'Here hold on to us,' she guided Mo's arms around their necks. The two older girls crossed their arms and clasping their hands together to create a basket to carry Mo home.

'What in the name of creation's the matter?' Mo's Granny greeted them at the door. 'What a racket I could hear you all the way down the road. *Shush, shush,*

shush. Come in quick before you shatter all the windows with that piercing greetin.' Granny's forehead creased into a frown.

'What's happened to her, Trisha?'

Once inside the kitchen she sat down at the kitchen table and sat Mo on to her knee.

'It's alright. It's alright,' she comforted, 'Calm down. Now tell me what happened?'

Unable to speak, Mo buried her head into her granny's neck smearing her with hot tears and snot. She bubbled, Trisha wouldn't let me...'

'It wasn't my fault.' Trish butted in indignantly. 'She fell when she was trying to skip.' Trisha was well used to her little sister's dramatics. 'She's only grazed her knee.' She said in a bored voice. 'Can I go back out to play now granny?'

'Aye on you go,' her granny sighed then turning back to Mo she crooned, 'For heaven's sake, wheesht bairn.'

Stroking Mo's hair she rocked her back and forth. 'Stop greetin' Mo,' She held her at arm's length and studied her with anxious eyes. 'Is yer knee sare?' Do you think you could stand up?'

Between hiccup sobs, Mo gulped.

'Ma knee IS sare Granny, but that's not why I'm crying. I was playing with the big girls. They were teaching me to skip. Kathleen Irvine cawed the rope too fast and it caught round my ankle.'

She looked at her granny with teary eyes and her face crumpled.

'I'm sorry,' her lip trembled. 'I dropped Hetty and her head got smashed.' She turned her eyes away not able to look at her granny's face. 'You said Hetty was YOUR dolly when you were wee and how she was very precious and I had to look after her very carefully. Now she's got broken and it's all my fault.' She burst into further floods of tears.

'Hush. It's not the end of the world. Stop your caterwaulin' you'll wake yer wee brother. Your mother's putting him down for a nap. Now let's tak a look at yer knee.'

Mo sat quietly whilst her granny took some liniment and cotton wool from the first aid box and gently dabbed and cleaned grit from the raw wound. Then, she wrapped a white gauze bandage around the injured knee.

'There you go wounded soldier. You'll mend.'

Just then Trisha burst in holding Mo's dolly wrapped in a mud splattered shawl.

'The back of her head's got busted, look granny,' she said, pulling a long face.

Her granny took a strip of white linen from her sewing table and hunting through the baby basket, she pulled out a nappy pin. '*Just the very dab.*'

'Give her over to me Trish.' She took the doll gently onto her knee and deftly wound the strip of linen around the doll's damaged head. 'Now if you hold this here for me,' she took Mo's finger and pressed it against the join of the bandage, 'I'll just pin it securely like this.' She pressed her lips together in concentration. 'There. Now she has a bandage too. I think you'll both do just fine.'

She passed the doll back to Mo who cradled Hetty in her arms. The doll's vacant blue eyes impassively gazed up at her, her rosebud painted lips revealing just the merest hint of a smile.

A piercing howl from the bedroom made Granny roll her eyes.

'That's a sare cry. Poor wee mite. Yer wee brother can't settle. I'm sure he's teething.' she tutted. 'There'll be no sleep for your mother again tonight.'

Mo tucked the shawl around her dolly.

'I'm a big sister now. Hetty and I can skip,' she whispered.

At a Distance

June 1995

She just lay there, slovenly sprawled out over the settee, with that crabbit look on her face.

'You're not going?' I asked.
'Nah.'

My wee sister's 40th birthday bash was looming. The whole family would turn out in force to celebrate. But my teenage daughter had no such plans. I made one last feeble attempt to change her mind.

'They'll be so disappointed if you don't turn up.'
'Sorry,' she shrugged.

She rose to her feet. As she walked out the front door to disappear down the garden path, I tried to fathom out this inexplicable change to her once uncomplicated, sunny, easy nature - now reticent, hostile and unapproachable. Our once good relationship had become increasingly disconnected. What's going on with her? It's not as if she's a young adolescent with raging hormones. She's 17. I felt at a loss. How could I try to fix things between us. I dislike the expression 'quality time' but I reasoned, maybe some time away together might help to bring us back closer together? Opportunities to talk were few but whilst giving her a lift in the car I took the chance to run an idea past her.

'Eve, how would you fancy going away for a few days just the two of us. I thought maybe the Lake District? Remember our lovely holidays there…' I caught her scornful look and rushed on, '…but you could choose where we go.'

'Ok.'

To my complete amazement she didn't rebuff me, she warmed to the idea.

'Yeah. I've been wanting to see Prague.'

Prague? I hadn't planned on going that kind of distance. It definitely wasn't one of the places I hankered to see. I imagined it to be an austere grim place, a throw-back to its 1968 Soviet occupation. However, since she was very keen to go, I agreed.

'Prague it is.'

No mobile phones, no internet to browse in those days. I arranged the flights through a travel agent and found an apartment advertised in the *Scotsman's* classified holiday-let columns. A two bedroom apartment within the heart of Prague centre.

'Perfect,' I thought as I dashed to send off a letter popping a cheque inside to book it.

'It's done,' I told my daughter with a mixture of excitement and trepidation. 'We're going to Prague!'

On the journey, we rekindled some of our old camaraderie and upon arrival at Vaclav Havel Airport, we were in high spirits. After exchanging our pounds sterling to Czech crowns, I hailed a taxi showing the driver the address tag attached to the apartment key I'd been sent. With a surly nod, he pulled out on to the auto-ban. Fifteen minutes on, as he sped away from the city, alarm bells began to ring.

'Where are you taking us?' How… far… from …the… city.. centre?' I made the usual tactless fauxpas of assuming if you speak slower to a foreigner, you'll be understood.

His indifferent shrug said it all. I realised that any attempt at conversation would be futile since I spoke no Czech and he evidently spoke no English.

'Is something wrong? Where is he taking us Mum?' my daughter picked up on my anxiety and sought to me for reassurance.

'No, nothing's wrong,' I said, hoping my confident tone would disguise my unease.

Peering out of the cab window a sickening feeling told me we were being taken in the opposite direction from the city centre. I'd checked the map to see where our apartment was located and was excited it was right in the heart of the Old Town, perfect for sightseeing on foot. I felt alarm bells. Why were we were being driven far, far out into the suburbs?

Eventually, we were dropped in the middle of an enormous development of monstrous ugly tower blocks.

'Thanks,' I muttered.

With shaky hands I thrust a wodge of notes at the driver, allowing him to help himself to his due (and more if he pleased 'cos I couldn't got my head around the currency).

Our hearts sank further as we stood outside, gazing up at the twenty floors of a mind-numbingly faceless tower block.

'Come on,' I said, gritting my teeth.

Whilst dragging my case inside the building, I felt rudely assaulted by the foul stink of pee in the foyer and the daggers my daughter aimed at me.

'Let's get our stuff up and get settled in, once we find our bearings it'll be fine.'

She shouldered her ruck-sack and gave me a withering look.

'The lift doesn't work. We'll have to take the stairs,' she informed me in a flat voice.

'You do have the key, don't you?' she nervously asked, slumping against the wall to take a much need breather on the 10th floor. 'Huh! That'll be the next catastrophe,' she snorted with derision.

Too out of breath to speak, I just nodded.

'Thank heavens,' I gasped as we reached the eleventh floor and passed by shabby nameless front doors. With a long breath, I was relieved.

'This is it. Apartment 11/99.'

Turning the key, we stepped inside warily. The interior was an unexpected revelation. Spacious, light filled and airy, the flat's 1960's décor both surprised and delighted us.

'Oooh look, it's a David Nightingale Hicks design.'

I stroked the psychedelic wallpaper's big bright yellow and pale green headed flowers, while admiring the pop-art posters! Eyes popping, I explored the rest of this retro apartment; shag rugs, huge paper lampshades, macramé baskets of spider plants hung in every corner. I felt as though I were tripping out! Best of all we discovered, the apartment's huge outside balcony which afforded a spectacular vista of Prague's distant skyline.

'Let's have a nosey in the kitchen,' I said, my disposition distinctly more cheerful.

'Yuk.' Eve scornfully observed. 'There's undies soaking in the sink and dirty dishes on the table.' She wrinkled her nose.

'Hmm.' I surveyed the mess. 'It looks to me like this flat's been vacated in a hurry! I think someone's making a bit of extra cash out of letting their home to us for the week-end.'

Setting to, we wrung out the washing and rinsed the crockery but at the sound of a key turning in the front door lock, we both froze wide-eyed in our tracks.

Four bewildered girls stood wedged in the kitchen doorway gawping at us. We gawped back.

'What are you doing here?' I stammered, bemused. We're renting this apartment for the weekend'. A tall blonde girl with pale blue eyes shook her head and responded in perfect English, 'We live in this apartment.'

The quartet huddled together in confab while we stood awkwardly, exchanging nervous looks and feeling powerless to do anything. They came to a decision. The blonde girl who apparently had the best command of English turned to us.

'I will go out to the street telephone box to speak to our landlord. Please wait here.' She indicated we should sit. We waited, fidgeting in an uncomfortable silence for what felt like ages. Finally, she returned.

'It's ok,' she smiled, allaying our fears. 'He apologises. There has been a bad mistake you were sent the wrong key with the wrong address. You will stay here with us tonight and tomorrow he will send a car for you.'

I could have hugged her.

'Thank You! Are you sure it's alright that we stay with you tonight? Do you have room for us? Should we try to find a hotel?'

Marija, her name transpired, briefly discussed the situation with the other girls and they kindly offered one of their bedrooms whilst the evicted girls would sleep on the sofas. After sleeping arrangements were settled, we shared their meagre meal of bread and salami. We were so hungry, no food had ever before tasted so good. Sitting round their kitchen table, sipping the Southern Comfort we had bought from the duty-free shop and sharing our monster bar of Cadburys chocolate we all began to relax and chat.

In conversation, we discovered they relocated from Zagreb, Yugoslavia. Their parents sent them to University in Prague to keep them safe from the bitter war being waged in their country. They were existing on very little money and just one proper meal a day which was provided by the University. They had no idea how long they would be away from their homes or when, or even if, they would ever see their families again. They only provided the briefest snap-shot of their lives but Eve and I felt we had formed a bond with those girls. Such a distance from home, cut adrift from their families.

The following day, a car arrived for us as promised. Hugging and thanking our short-term hosts, we scribbled down our home address for them but realistically, and sadly, accepted it was unlikely we'd ever see them again. We wished them the best of luck as we departed.

Our driver dropped us at a quaint central apartment situated on Wenceslas Square's wide boulevard in the heart of Prague's charming centre. Over the next couple of days, Eve and I wandered the city's ancient streets and squares, it's unfolding magnificence truly taking our breath away. On our last night, sitting together on the balcony of our apartment and marvelling at the stunning sun-set, my daughter fixed troubled eyes on me.

'Mum, I've been wanting to talk to you about something. Well it's..' she blurted out, '…I want you to know I'm gay.'

I nodded.

'I know. I think I've always known. But ***honestly*** it doesn't have to be a big thing, does it Eve? You're no different today than you were yesterday… just be happy being the lovely person you are….'

Upon arriving home in Edinburgh, I hastily sent cash in an envelope to the girls' address in Prague, in the heartfelt hope, it would somehow make life a little easier for them. I often thought about them; so young, so brave, so kind. Living such a long way from their homes and separated from their families, and with none of today's technology to breach that distance. I wondered what became of them.

Some years later, I lifted mail from my front porch and examined an air-mail envelope with an unexpected Croatian postmark. It was a letter from Marija.

Lockdown Entanglement

R ose flirted coquettishly on the WhatsApp vid.

'So? Chuck?' she probed.

Without hesitation he responded with a blushing wink and an air kiss.

'…don't see why not!'

How fortunate, he pondered, to find the ravishing Rose in the autumn of his life. Truly. A perfect match through the TINDR ad he posted –

Intelligent well-dressed gentleman widower mid-70s folically blessed N/S GSOH. Interests art, gardening, fine dining WLTM special lady.

Chuck was like a pubescent, cock-a-hoop schoolboy when first they spoke online. Their first date was on the last Sunday of February when they met at The Dome, a favourite romantic rendezvous in Edinburgh. The Club Room's candlelit fine diner was perfect. Rose shimmied over to his table, emitting that *je ne sais quoi* charm when they first met face to face.

'Hello Chuck,' she said coyly with a well-spoken Edinburgh lilt.

The slim, attractive strawberry-blonde did not appear her 63 years. Hypnotic blue eyes, immaculately eye-lined, and inviting pouty cupid lips – simply irresistible. Chemistry struck instantly.

Their comfortable chit-chat continued over Chuck's breakfast table the next morning. He was lovestruck. Those unexpected midnight flames of passion, were all but forgotten from a distant past. With daily WhatsApp contact and another couple of dates, things were going very well indeed.

Overwhelmed in the blossoming romance, Chuck somehow missed the mounting urgency reported on the BBC headline news: the worsening Covid-19 pandemic. So, Nicola Sturgeon's shock announcement of imperative lockdown guidelines for over 70s hit like a thunderbolt. ***Self-isolate. Keep social distance.***

Chuck instinctively knew moving in together was premature. It was still in the early flush of their relationship: but a no-brainer nevertheless.

24ᵗʰ March

DAY 1

Rose arrived on his doorstep - laden with four huge suitcases, a cat, it's basket, it's litter tray and … her freckled 10 year old grand-daughter Erica! Bewildered, Chuck politely accepted Rose's apologetic explanation that as her daughter who lives at home shows symptoms, Rose and Erica must stay safe. And Molly the pussy with her pink bejewelled collar suffers separation anxiety without Rose – and it seems vice versa.

Chuck recalled their previous chit-chat. Molly and Erica's existence never arose, but then again, he didn't divulge his knee osteoarthritis - nor FELINE allergy. So, gentlemanly Chuck 'welcomed' them all. Milk for

Molly, Irn Bru for Erica, a red wine for Rose and a very large stiff Glenmorangie for himself.

A cloud of doom was descending.

DAY 2

Erica's behaviour, sulks and rudeness had escalated. The harder Chuck tried to placate her, the worse her tantrums heightened. Her boredom was damned testing.

DAY 3

Rose suggested a wee shopping trip to Tesco. Chuck, whose red swollen eyes were bulging like ping pong balls whilst nursing a dull headache which hurt with every sneeze, enthusiastically agreed.

'Get that wee sulky scunner out of my sight,' he thought.

'Here's my debit card and pin number Rose. Go take Erica and get some groceries,' he offered.

But arriving home in a taxi a couple of hours later with umpteen bags of shopping, proving him £270.21 poorer, he was visibly taken aback. Activity set with pens and chalk, twelve tins Whiskas chicken liver,

Loreal beauty products plus two blouses and a Kenwood liquidiser - all amongst the ***grocery*** haul.

Upon mention of the extravagance, Rose smiled sweetly and cupping her hands on his handsome but now rash-ridden face, she scolded him for being miserly. He said nothing more but decided he'd not be her sugar daddy nor ever let his debit card out of his sight again.

DAY 4

His crowded home meant the days passed s-l-o-w-l-y … and painfully. Rose prattled incessantly on the phone to *god knows who* whilst filing her nails, clipping her toenails or waxing her legs. Cooking and cleaning for ungrateful guests was galling.

Glued to BBC news, Chuck ***prayed*** for a lockdown lift.

DAY 5

Erica's Karaoke machine, delivered by Amazon and courtesy of his debit card details, **blared loudly**!

DAY 6

Upon his morning retreat to his back garden with cuppa in hand, Chuck was blinded by *that* eyesore. He blinked in disbelief. The rear wall, the patio slabs and his precious man shed now featured unsightly rainbow graffiti hues of pink, yellow, orange and blue **chalk!**

DAY 7

Before the opportunity arose to raise his ever-growing list of woes with Rose, she commanded another Tesco jaunt. Apparently, soap and toilet rolls were top of the shopping list. This time, they ALL set off. Defying isolating rules, a puffy-eyed, sneezing Chuck, despondently limped with his walking stick aid, scuffling behind a sprightly Rose. Her brightly painted nails adorned her long soft fingers which held on tightly to Erica's hand.

It was a testy, impatient twenty-minute wait in the social distancing queue before Rose burst into the store like a contestant on Supermarket Sweep. She hurriedly hurled stuff into the trolley - while Chuck slyly tried (in vain) to return as much as he could to the shelves.

'Oh look!' she exclaimed. 'Toilet rolls!'

She rushed towards the solitary remaining pack. OOPS. Too late. A competitive shopper's hand swooped in.

That was when Chuck encountered a Rose less sweet. Possessed in mounting wrath, expletives flowed freely. A brawl ensued with her equally frustrated challenger shopper - pushing, shoving, hair pulling. Astonished, Chuck could only gape in horror as Rose grabbed his walking stick and repeatedly whacked, not only the toilet roll 'thief' but also, the intervening security staff.

Within minutes, Police Scotland, were called. Witness statements were taken and on account of the presiding social distancing rules, the warring culprits were transported in separate cars to Gayfield Police Station. A lengthy three hours later Rose was facing a charge of assault. Worse still, Chuck's walking stick was confiscated - as evidence!

ROSE HAD TO GO!

He diplomatically suggested she return home but one word led to another 'til a stormy row brewed thick and strong. Her heated response left him flummoxed. With eyeliner and lipstick smudged and painted nails chipped and broken, her ladylike demeanour had vanished.

'I cannae ging hame Sunshine! Ma' contagious daughter's isolating wi' ma' husband. Me, ma' grandchild and ma' cat are gan naewhere!'

Chuck despairingly reflected, '*What husband?*'

Jean Jeannie: Let Yourself Go

S andrine's Hair & Beauty Salon looked too posh for Jean.

She preferred to let Lorna, her local hairdresser give her a trim, but Jean often wondered, when she was handing over a £2 tip, what part of *'Don't take much off'*, did Lorna not understand.

Maybe she would just take a look in to Sandrine's to check if they did ear piercing? The Celtic earrings were pretty. Hiding her disappointment, she'd thanked Robbie for his gift as she lied, 'They're a perfect choice.' But Jean had felt irritated. It was typical of Robbie not to realise, after all their years together, she didn't have pierced ears

The teenager sitting at Sandrine reception gave her the once over and peeking through a sheath of perfectly coiffed blond hair informed her, in a slightly superior tone.

'No, sorry…' she shook her mane, '…we don't do piercing.'

Jean was almost out the door when she turned back.

'Would you have anyone free now who could give me a haircut?'

'Can do!' the girl replied in a friendlier tone. 'We've just had a cancellation. Raymond could take you in 10 minutes if you can wait?'

'Is he good at cutting hair, dear?' Jean asked.

Arching her perfect tattooed eyebrows, the receptionist gave a snooty look.

'Raymond is a Senior Salon Director madam, so YES, of course he's an excellent hair technician. But everyone here has a superb reputation for hair styling, Madam!'

She flicked her eyes indicating the direction of the waiting area. 'Please take a seat.'

As Jean leafed through a Vogue magazine, searching for inspiration, a junior stylist who was wearing far too much make-up, in her opinion, approached and took her anorak. The youngster plainly showed distaste at the garment.

After being gowned, she was seated in front of a brightly lit wall mirror, to wait for the expert hair stylist to materialise. From her reflection, she scrutinised her appearance – it had been ages since she'd done this. Sat there, it was unavoidable and she realised how old she looked! When had her eyes become hooded and baggy, her mouth wrinkled, a brow frown so lined, her jaw line slack and, she noted with dismay, a soft paunchy roll under her chin? But it was her hair which aged her the most; lank, lifeless greying and badly cut.

Two hands pressing on her shoulders startled her. The young slim, tanned, dark haired lad's reflection studied her, assessing her in the mirror.

'Jean?' he flashed a row of super white teeth, 'what can I do for you today?'

Jean hesitated then nodded at the reflection.

'Truthfully, I don't really know what I want but I do know what I DON'T want. I don't want to look like THIS!'

Raymond patted her shoulder gently.

'No problem my darlin' we can fix this. Your hair's quite short but we could texturize it. Hmm…' he scrunched his fingers through her barnet, '…we could create a more modern funky look. How would that be?'

Jean smiled. 'Yes, sounds good.'

'And colour?' Raymond asked, continuing running his fingers through her mop, pulling it into soft peaks.

'Yup, I definitely want to do something about the grey.'

'No problemo!' Raymond said in a jokey tone. 'Grey away.'

Raymond's manner was reassuring and Jean felt she could confide in him. Eyeing him in the mirror, she flushed a little.

'I turned 60 today,' she announced.

'Hey?' He grinned. 'You said that as if you were confessing to something shameful!'

Squeezing her shoulder he spun her chair. 'Listen to my wise words...'

'Age, is like glasses of wine, and should never be counted!'

'Right? Let's get to it. We could give you a brown rinse which would take you back to where you were,

OR, stroking his chin thoughtfully, if you feel brave enough we could just keep the grey and I could give you silver highlights and maybe just the merest flash of colour.'

'Flash of colour?' Jean wrinkled her nose, 'what kind of colour?'

'Well.' Raymond's eyes sized her up. 'When my Mum felt she needed a change I gave her a brand new look.' He lifted a small section of Jean's hair. 'We went for a bright red streak at the front,' his eyes lit up, '…it looks amazing!'

He continued, 'I think maybe for you though, a touch of blue, with just a flash of fuchsia.' He rested a hand on his hip and nodded. 'Yes, I think that could look really fabulous.'

Eyes widened, Jean retorted, 'I wouldn't have thought in my wildest dreams of having something like that…but maybe it's time to be bold. YEAH!' She gave a half-shrug and nodded, 'You only get one life, right? Go for it!'

'Grrreat. Good decision!' Raymond rubbed his hands together, 'Just you relax there a sec' lovie whilst I mix up your colour.'

Jean pressed her hand to her cheek and stared back.

'*Oh God. Am I doing the right thing? There's still time to change my mind,*' she thought.

Raymond was back in a trice and before Jean could say STOP, he performed his coiffure magic, spreading the purple paste over the strands of her hair.

'Now I'm going to leave you to *cook*,' he quipped, '…here's some mags to browse. Would you like a coffee lovie?'

Jean shook her head. Her stomach turned as she felt queasy with nerves. What the holy heck was she doing? She flicked through the magazines without concentrating.

Once *cooked*, the junior led her to a row of gleaming white sinks where she was dye rinsed and shampooed then subjected to a hugely uncomfortable head massage. Wearing a big fluffy towel on her head, she awaited the return of hair magician, Raymondo.

As he removed the towel and began to work scissor wonder, re-styling her hair, Jean lowered her eyes, too scared to check out her new image in the mirror. A blow dry and some hairspray, it was now finished. He held up a hand mirror so she could appraise the transformation.

Jean gasped at the now younger, punkier, funkier, kick-ass kinda lady. With a backward glimpse of the past, she was reminded of a young girl with a zig zag painted face, dancing at a David Bowie concert.

Expressing her delight, she gave Raymond a huge tip and made her next appointment.

'I'll definitely be coming back,' she grinned to the haughty unimpressed receptionist who was still peering through that annoying sweep of blonde fringe.

'Delighted you're happy madam,' she said in an artificially sugary voice. 'Would you like some product today?'

'No, not today thanks but do you happen to know of a shop anywhere near where I can get my ears pierced?' Jean asked.

'Ink-sperations in Forbes Street, round the corner,' she muttered sourly.

Without ado, Jean found the tattoo parlour and timidly tapped on the door behind the unmanned reception desk. Music was blaring from within. Her enquiring 'Hello?' brought forth a huge hulk of a lad who had multiple ear, nose and eyebrow piercings.

'*He looks s-c-a-r-y,*' Jean thought.

'I wondered if you do ear piercing?' Jean asked uncertainly. She looked past him and couldn't help but stare at a half-naked young man lying outstretched on a wide bench in the tattoo studio.

The hulk's reply was much friendlier than his appearance.

'Aye we do, that's Michelle. She's doon stairs wi' a client. She'll be up in a mo'. Huv a seat. She'll nae be long.' He disappeared back into the studio to tend to his undressed client.

Jean sat in the skull ornamented waiting room listening to the drilling of the big guy's art taking shape. Idly flicking through a book of tattoo designs, a thought struck her.

'Hell! Why Not?' she laughed out loud.

A dog collared, heavily tattooed Michelle who was adorning black lipstick, emerged.

'Yes Mam. What can I help you with? Is it ear-piercing?' she asked in a drawling tone whilst eyeing Jean's new hairdo with her theatrical, khol-crayoned eyes.

'Yes,' Jean nodded, '...and I was thinking of having this done,' pointing to a picture in the tattoo album.

Heading home, Jean felt a frisson of excitement. She felt more alive than she had in a LONG time.

Robbie had never been good at hiding his feelings and his expression displayed bemusement.

'Jean!' he gawked, '...is this MY Jean?'

Jean laughed, pushing past him through the door as she spun him a quote,

> *'When I am an old woman, I shall wear purple*
> *With a red hat which doesn't go, and doesn't suit me.*
> *And I shall spend my pension on brandy and summer gloves*
> *And satin sandals, and say we've no money for butter...'*

'Eh?' he shrugged, staring after her. 'Now you've got me flummoxed.'

'I'm quoting from a Jenny Joseph's poem Robbie,' Jean continued.

> *'...But maybe I ought to practise a little now?*
> *So people who know me are not too shocked and surprised,*
> *When suddenly I am old, and start to wear purple.'*

Jean proudly raked her fingers though her silver and heliotrope hair, with a sigh, 'Maybe I just needed a change Robbie. Do you like the new me?'

Robbie pulled at his ear, a habit of his when he pondered on something.

'Aye,' he nodded, slowly pulling Jean towards him, '…and I liked the old Jean too, mind. Touching her cheek gently, his brown eyes looked quizzically into hers.

'You're a smasher Jean Jeanie, but now you've got me thinking. Should I do something about *this?*'

Stroking his white beard, he teased, 'Maybe I should get it striped green, Eh? Up the HIBEES!'

Jean laughed out loud, punching him lightly on the shoulder, as she anticipated his shocked coupon when she'd later reveal her tattoo

.

The 1960s Easter Bunny

Aberdeen 1966

*B*unny *was a stripper, she worked on Friday nights,*
The money came in handy to keep her finances
right.
In stiletto heels, she flounced and writhed, she really was a
teaser,
To entertain boozy punters and all the sweaty geezers.

Her sexy pout with red ruby lips was part of her routine,
Her classy moves were tasteful, and not at all obscene.
In the wings, big bro' Sandy stood, scary with no charm,
Her roadie, her bouncer and taxi driver, protecting her
from harm.

Alluring lady in shimmering gold, she shed her glam attire
And when her nylons and suspenders came off, she set the club on fire.
She threw them to the audience, they soared off through the air,
Apart from skimpy panties, she was altogether bare.

The music gradually gathered pace, it really was toe curling
When her fluffy bobtail gyrated fast, spinning round and whirling.

The stripper held the men agape, her sleek body a sight to see,
Tanked up on all the whisky and beer, psyched up by her 36D.
Pumped up in their fantasy, the punters wildly cheered
But they could look and NEVER touch; from Sandy they were feart.

Elsie was a widow, with two kids at home with gran,
The scooter crash caused sore heartache, when she lost her
man.
Weekdays she worked forty hours, on Tinnies factory
floor,
Her weekly wage was counted out, to keep wolves from
the door.
A monotonous job, she toiled away, it was her bread and
butter,
For Elsie it was necessity, to save her family from the
gutter.

On Fridays there was usual chat, for the workforce of all
ages,
Excitement of the weekend, and how to spend their
meagre wages.
With scarves tied back at the nape of their necks, their
curlers partly hidden,
A tucked-in tranny could often be heard, even though it
was forbidden.

The 5 o'clock horn would finally blow, then a stampede through the gate,
In anticipation of a big night out, or for a romantic date.

Her factory pals were savvy, but clearly had no insight,
Where shy Elsie would frequent, or get up to on Friday night.
Elsie was a factory girl but nobody ever knew;
They'd never guess in a hundred years, what she could get up to.

Saturday morn, she'd wash off the slap with intense regularity
False lashes peeled, blonde wig packed – no trace of double identity.
Then after breakfast and dishes washed, the kids were dressed and waiting,
Hand in hand with loving mum, off to Donalds Ice Rink Skating.

*On Sundays, it was off to kirk, (at Easter it was
crammed),
Altogether in their Sunday best with bibles in their
hands.*

*No glitzy glamorous beauty was she, not so sophisticated;
Her recognition of faces in the pews, was not reciprocated.
Of her secret she'd wryly smile, she thought it mildly
funny,
These pious men were unaware, SHE was their Easter
Bunny.*

Table for Tosh at 7.30

The short, smartly-dressed lady with the pink streak in her black, bobbed hair appeared from nowhere.

'Table for Tosh at 7.30?'

Bridget raised her eyes from the busy Saturday night reservation chart which she had been reviewing as she squeezed in yet another table booking. She recognised this customer. A few hours earlier during lunchtime service, dressed in a track suit resembling un-ironed pyjamas and minus the fancy hairdo, she rushed in like a whirlwind to drop off an exceedingly large, scrumptious chocolate birthday cake for her husband. With a warm smile, Bridget welcomed the party.

'Good evening', she offered, then picking up six dinner menus, she showed the guests to Table 9, a spacious round table by the door which was ready and waiting for their arrival.

The restaurant was already filling up fast and Bridget found it hard sometimes not to panic a little as she anticipated the ensuing madness lying in wait of a busy Saturday night ahead. Mrs Tosh shrugged her disapproval of Table 9 and with a nod and a finger point, she signalled her preference to Table 2, even though it was only seated for five. With customer care at the heart of their small but successful operation, this was no problem. Bridget quickly beckoned Katy.

'Please set up Table 2 with an additional setting.'

No sooner said than done, the birthday boy, his dinner mates and his bossy little wife were comfortably seated, perusing the Mediterranean menu.

The wonderful aroma of herbs and spices – basil, oregano, cumin, coriander, tarragon – wafted from the open Turkish kitchen where Bridget's hubby Zafer was joking in his mother tongue with his kitchen brigade.

'*Probably about Galatasaray's winning game over Besiktas,*' she guessed while rolling her eyes.

After decades in Aberdeen as a near solitary Turk, the daily Turkish chit chat in his new Edinburgh restaurant was still a novelty for him.

'*What's he got to laugh about?*' she pondered as she recalled THAT incident earlier in the day.

In between meeting and greeting, Bridget would scuttle back to her domain behind the bar where the drinks orders and call for bills were fast amounting. This was HER hub where she'd serve the drinks; answer the telephone; take reservations; tend to the ice machine; fill and empty the glass washer; 'orchestrate' the table service team, all amongst a host of other tasks.

'*As if I don't do enough, he's now suggesting I could fortune tell the customers' Turkish coffee cups too,*' she chuckled to herself, '*he's such a joker!*'

The restaurant service team comprising her well-trained reliable 'gals', were all hand-picked at recruitment - not for waiting experience but for their work ethic, polite personalities and willingness to learn. Sometimes Bridget likened herself *to Miss Jean Brodie in her Prime.*

This was in stark contrast to Zafer's 'evlatlari' who at times Bridget found nearly impossible to manage. In fact, she felt relieved if the chefs turned up for work in time and bothered to comb their hair or shave before their shifts. It was funny, she thought, how around 11pm each Saturday night, they strutted out the door together to hit the Edinburgh night life - suited and booted like John Travoltas, perfectly groomed with gelled quiffs and a whiff of Lynx.

The restaurant opened around two months previously with no grand opening ceremony, no expensive PR marketing campaign and no hefty advertisement bill. Zafer drew on his 30+ years experience in hotel hospitality management, opting for a gentle start into the brand new food and service operation. Important, he decided, for the team to get acquainted with the menu and the operation system.

'Money is better spent to invest in the customers. Word of mouth recommendation is the key to ongoing success. Once customers are

*through the door, it's the vital opportunity to
keep them happy to ensure they return'.*

And of-course he was right.

But one Tuesday evening, barely a month after the new restaurant opened its freshly painted doors, a local grande dame strolled in without warning or reservation seeking a table for herself and a friend. Gillian Glover was a prominent, well known *Scotsman on Sunday* food critic whose sharp, witty and often cutting reviews could close a new start eaterie with a singular swiping remark. From Ms Glover's entertaining beautifully written articles, she was a foodie goddess. Although her visit was intended to be *anonymous*, Zafer immediately recognised the dark-haired bespectacled lady from her profile pic on her weekly review page. In a moment of inspiration, Bridget had cut out the photo and sellotaped it to the till.

What Zafer lacked in head hair, he oozed in debonair charm and that night he laid it on thick.

'Oh my god, did everything go well? Did she complain?' Bridget quizzed him the following morning, wishing she had been on duty.

'No complaint and she looked happy', he retorted confidently.

The next few days dragged on and on. With bated breath they waited for the Sunday paper's big reveal. And there it was. The headline read – '**God must be Turkish!**'.

Wow! Like only a connoisseur could, she described the Hunkar Begendi, tender succulent lamb with orgasmic aubergine creamed sauce to mouth-watering acclaim and compared Cankaya white wine to a fine Chardonnay. She recounted the freshly made melt in the mouth baklava pastries drenched in sweet rose honey syrup and sprinkled with chopped pistachio. Service, décor and ambience were all highly favourable – nothing not to like. Well that was it. From that day forward, the telephone reservation enquiries poured in. The 'celebrity' reviewer's recommended lamb dish and white wine was a firm favourite for fans of the foodie queen. Yes, the couple owed a lot to dear Gillian and to be fair she became an occasional customer for the next ten years – albeit a slightly risky one!

A few months earlier, Zafer set wheels in motion to open his first restaurant business, so different from corporate hotel management in which he was employed all his working life. It was a real shame that he couldn't find premises in Aberdeen where for 25 years he built an enviable reputation as a popular and well respected Maitre D and hospitality manager. His relocation to Edinburgh meant leaving a valuable and sizeable list of clientele and contacts behind, to start afresh in a new city. His longstanding *'friend'*, a fellow Turk, persuaded him that it would be beneficial if he'd be Zafer's 'sleeping' partner', not to mention supplier of foodstuffs from his butchery and food factory in Aberdeen. And Zafer need never worry about paperwork, he claimed, because his accountants would process everything including banking and wages. For Zafer, it sounded too good to be true – and therein lies a warning! It was! But that's perhaps a story for another day!

In the first couple of weeks of opening, for three days running, a gang of young Turks bombarded the premises. They mistook the restaurant for a Kahvehane (a Turkish coffee house), a rendezvous where they could hang out. This was not good news. Their presence created unpleasant smoky cigarette haze, loud banter and unsociable behaviour. They propped their filthy trainers on the brand new upholstered chairs – one time, even on a table top beside the cutlery. To allow this to continue was unthinkable. Zafer and the kitchen team were wary about how to tackle the invasion.

First day, chef (who had invited them) had a quiet word with them. But they returned.

Second day, Zafer diplomatically suggested they leave. But they returned.

Third day, Bridget… well, she had no such reservations. Smiling sweetly, and before the rowdy crew had time to contemplate, they were shown the door and evicted from the premises to the street below. That's when the malicious and threatening phone calls began.

'We smash your window glasses, son of a donkey!'

'We watch you, you bears!'

'We cook you like kebabs, you cucumbers!'

Hoax reservations resulted in no-shows. And the outdoor plants often took a revenge hit as they were midnight 'watered'. The ugly campaign seemed to go on forever.

This particular Saturday, just after three o'clock, Bridget proceeded to climb the steep cobbles of Howe Street, which she often breathlessly nicknamed Kilimanjaro. Nipping home, after the lunchtime stint, to freshen up and have a cuppa, she would return to the 'shop' at 5pm to open for the evening shift. But a touch of afternoon retail therapy was always welcome before opening for business - a browse around Karen Millen, Coast and Hobbs. Approaching George Street, she noted their premises was in darkness and sussed that Zafer must have closed up shop after the last lunchtime customers left. He's probably checking out the odds at Ladbrokes, she assumed.

It was then she spied them. Two young dark haired lads, scurrying up the restaurant steps towards the glass front door. She halted in her tracks. From the opposite side of the street, she waited, she waited, she waited – but they were gone.

'*Oh - my - god,*' she fretted, '*they are in the restaurant.*'
'*Must've broken in.*'
'*Who are they?*'

'*What are they doing in there?*'
'*Would she call the police?*'

Cautiously, she crossed the road to investigate - but there was no sign of them. Heart pounding, she climbed the steps and as she slowly turned the brass door handle and peeked inside, she spied two uninvited strangers sitting quietly on Table 14 – with no lights on, the empty restaurant was dark and silent. Scared stiff, she approached tentatively, wishing she could ditch her high heels for trainers.

'Can I help you?' she muttered.

'Yes. Please bring two Efes beers and a couple of menus,' they courteously replied. All innocent.

It suddenly dawned that her darling overworked hubby had simply forgotten to lock the door. She rolled her eyes.

The afternoon's scary event was never far from her thoughts this Saturday evening. By half past nine, the restaurant was buzzing and as well-fed, well-watered happy diners left, new hungry customers arrived, some she already identified as regulars. The din and hilarity was near-deafening. Even Turkish pop idol

Tarkan's version of *Kiss Kiss* could barely be heard through the Sony speakers.

The Tosh's party cake was waiting patiently beside the kitchen server when Zafer ushered the team to follow him and join in with the infamous *Happy Birthday* ditty. All diners looked on in amusement. But to Bridget's horror, the sparkly candle lit cake bypassed Table 2. Confusion splattered over Mrs Tosh's face, as she wondered where the hell her cake was going. She didn't have to wait long before she saw it ceremoniously presented to Table 9, where the guests laughed, clapped and cheered at the unexpected treat.

Bridget held on tightly to her composure as she shouted over the din to Zafer.

'There's been a mistake. The cake's on the wrong table'.

'Ne?'' he replied.

Sidling up beside him, she cupped her hands to his ear.

'The bloody cake is on the wrong f***ing table.'

When he spied the pink striped haired customer's animated face, he nervously stroked his moustache.

Meantime, Table 9 were having a field day demolishing the hi-jacked piece of chocolate art as they coshed in with the pasta knife. Bridget calmly whisked the cake ruins off to the kitchen while deliberately avoiding eye contact with the furious Table 2 diners.

A quick confab with the team, the recouping plan was agreed. Her explanation and apology to Table 9 was duly accepted in good humour, especially with the round of free liqueurs that followed.

Head chef restructured the chocolate treat by cementing it together with freshly whipped cream, and adding embellishment of fresh fruit and an all-important freshly lit candle. Zafer appeased the Toshes with an especially raucous rendition of *Happy Birthday* at which the whole restaurant chorused in as he energetically clapped and danced – well, a kinda dad version of a belly dance.

The *'büyük hata'* was forgiven by Mrs Tosh and all's well that ends well, especially after TWO complimentary rounds of after-dinner drinks AND a free bottle of wine!

The patrons were happy and that's what counts.

As midnight approached, all tables had by now already paid and most had vacated, hopefully to return another time. Only a couple of parties still lingered as they savoured the ambience. Tired and exhausted after a hectic Saturday night and with feet stinging like hell, Bridget was in her hub, cashing up and longing to cast aside her kitten heels and sip a glass of well-deserved vino.

Trying hard to keep straight faces, two of her *'gals'*, Katy and Laura, crept up to the bar arm in arm as they stifled their giggles. Katy then relayed the *amusing* message to *'Ms Brodie'*.

'Zafer says, 'Please go to Table 2 to read the lady's coffee cup"

Afiyet Olsun!

Sorry Babe

He turned to Shona as he took the call on the bedroom balcony.   'Sorry babe, I've got to take this.'

Hanging her clothes on a temporary rail he'd rigged up, she wondered if he would mind her taking one of his bedroom drawers to store her underwear. Better wait and ask him she decided. He'd already shown irritation when she'd moved his shoes without permission, to make room for hers in his wardrobe. How could a man have so many pairs of shoes?

She quashed the tiny doubts that still niggled at the back of her mind. Had she done the right thing giving up her good job and lovely rented flat in Glasgow, to move her whole life down to London, just to be with him? She'd only known him a couple of months. It wasn't like her to make impulsive decisions but he was so charming, so good looking, so successful, so perfect. The first time he asked her out, she was flabbergasted. What on earth did he see in dowdy shy plain-Jane Shona? Unbelievably, after a wonderful and passionate couple of months she found herself pregnant. When he immediately asked her to marry him, she'd felt ecstatic.

'No point in waiting to have a big showy do,' he'd said. 'Let's get hitched, just the two of us. More romantic,' he'd whispered, kissing her neck. 'We don't have to find a bigger place just yet. You can move into mine for the time being. It's perfect,' he decided.

As Shona reflected on the whirlwind events that had upended her whole life, Jonathon startled her by silently coming up behind her. Wrapping his arms around her pinning her arms to her side.

'Just leave that 'til later babe.' He lifted the clothes she'd spread out on the bed and shoved them back into her case.

'I hate untidiness, never could stand it. By the way, that was my mother calling. She's organised a garden luncheon party. Just a small soirée. Get dressed. Wear something suitable.'

He slid along the dresses she'd hung on the rail and with a nod of his head made his selection.

'Yup this green one'll do. Get ready, it's a bit of a drive across to Beckenham.'

'Do we have to go Jonathon?' she gently protested. 'I've only just arrived. I thought we could spend the weekend together, just the two of us.'

'Sorry babe,' he replied in a clipped tone. 'My mother wants to meet you. It's a command performance!'

She felt his tension as they drove across London.

'Are you alright Jonathon. You're very quiet,' she ventured.

'Just work babe. I'm just distracted thinking about bloody work. Sorry. Look, we're nearly there.'

He turned the car into a grand, tree-lined avenue of large red bricked mock Tudor mansions. They drove through heavy security gates and up a sweeping driveway to the front of the impressive residence. One of the hired staff approached and took the keys to park the car.

Shona could feel herself growing nervous. She had no idea his family lived in such an upmarket wealthy area. They were ushered into a light airy reception area and offered wine and canapes by waiters in dark suits who were hovering around the guests. She had never felt so isolated amongst so many people.

Jonathon was immediately whisked away by a thin blonde woman who wiggled her way over towards them wearing a tight black dress and red killer high heels.

'You don't mind, do you darling?' she stated linking her arm through Jonathon's and giving Shona a brittle smile. 'Jonathon and I have so much to catch up on, don't we poppet?' She gave him a flirtatious smile.

Guests milled around Shona, drinks in hands. Some occasionally shifted their gaze towards her then gave her a quick appraisal before looking away with disinterest. She stood on the side lines whilst the carefully coiffed females formed groups, interacting easily with each other, so obviously long- time friends. Their indifferent spouses discussed cars, wine and sport. Kids raced around creating chaos, their shrieks and screams and tantrums painful to the ears.

Shona looked nervously at the cliques and had no idea where she fitted in. Taking a deep breath, she thought she should probably try to circulate.

'So, you're the little Scotch girl Jonathon's taken up with, are you?' said an overweight elderly lady with wispy grey hair. Wearing a white silk kaftan and far too much rouge, she bore down on her. Without giving Shona a chance to respond she continued in an imperious voice.

'I'm Gloria, Jonathon's mother.'

Her pale blue eyes drilled into Shona's.

'It's high time that boy settled down to a quiet life. Needs a steadying influence. Wasn't ever going to work out with Sybil. She didn't want to give him children you know? Have you ever heard anything so ludicrous? I always thought she was a flighty piece and told him so. I said, '*Jonathon, if you don't settle down and have children I'm cutting you out of my will.*' He knew I meant it. But of-course he was mad for her. Blinded by passion. He wouldn't listen to me. I'm only his mother.'

She hardly paused to take a breath.

'But at last, after all this time it seems he **has** listened to me and come to his senses. He married you. I do hope you plan to have lots of babies.'

She hesitated in her diatribe, spotting a tall woman waving and heading over in their direction who was trying to catch her eye.

'Daphne dear. How kind of you to come to my little lunch to celebrate Jonathon's nuptials. Yes dear, they got married in Scotland. They wanted it to be a very quiet affair. No fuss. Do meet Jonathon's bride.'

Something about the way she said '*bride*' conveyed to Shona a certain cynicism.

'Excuse me won't you, I have to go and supervise in the kitchen or lunch will be a most ghastly disaster.' She sailed away like a stately Spanish galleon.

Shona felt a flush of colour rise to her cheeks. She stood tongue tied, lost for words whilst snooty Daphne gave her a long cold stare examining her as if she were an unusual species of insect. A waiter pushed a silver tray of canapes under Shona's nose. She looked at the little rounds of pastry smeared with black oily sludge and felt a wave of nausea rise up in her throat. She felt the room swirl. At that awful moment, she realised that she was going to pass out.

In a swirl of red mist she crumpled to the floor. Lying in half consciousness, she heard the voices of women whisper above her, as if from a distance.

'Daphne dear, what happened? Should we call a doctor? Should we fetch Jonathon?'

'Someone, get her some water. There's probably no need for a doctor. Maybe I shouldn't say, but she's in early pregnancy. Quite common to faint at that stage, don't you know?'

'You mean he's got her pregnant already? My God he's a fast worker. I heard the rumours of course. Gloria giving him the ultimatum. She told him she would disinherit him, didn't she? Said she didn't care if he carried on with Sybil but she wanted grandchildren. Told him it was time he got himself a broodmare. Where on earth is Jonathon?' she craned her neck, 'I can't see him anywhere.'

'Daphne dear don't be silly. Do you really have to ask?' was the bitchy reply.

Shona felt strong arms raising her up. She opened her eyes to see Jonathon leaning over her. She could see he wasn't happy.

'What the hell happened. God you've made me look stupid.'

He lifted her and plonked her on a chair. Someone handed him water.

'Here. Sip this,' he instructed.

'Jonathon, can we go home please. I don't feel well,' Shona pleaded. She hated that all eyes were on her.

But he shook his head with impatience and she caught his derisory expression. Then he turned to someone standing at her shoulder, someone thin and blonde. Shona heard him mutter to her.

'Sorry babe.'

Letter from Winnipeg: Prelude

Brechin, Scotland 1917

Softly spoken Ina was the eldest of five sisters, all still living at home with their ma 'n da. The daily catty spats and din was overwhelming at times but Ina was a peaceful presence – a solitary white lily in a bed of prickly thistles. Her ambitious siblings opted to work as day girls with the gentry and flatly refused to work in the local dirty, dust fume filled workhouse, namely the Jute Works. But Ina accepted the inevitability of hard work wage earning sufferance, to contribute to her ma's housekeeping tin. She also accepted that her plain looks would not attract a *Prince Charming* and she was resigned to remaining a spinster for the rest of her life.

When Drew Marr started work at the factory, and paid unexpected attention to shy Ina, she was head over heels smitten. He wooed her with sweet romantic verses to express his love, and win her over; they married in 1918.

'When the golden sun is setting

And your mind from care is free;

When others you are thinking of,

Will you sometimes think of me?

Never forget me little darling,

Even though we're set apart;

And in the depths of thine affection

Will I gain your loving heart?

Think of me when you are happy,

Keep for me one little spot;

In the depth of thine affection

Plant the seed of forget me not.'

Anon

Letter from Winnipeg

Brechin, Scotland 1925

The Spring sunshine danced and sparkled over the rippling South Esk River as regal swans elegantly paddled downstream and the ducks dived amongst the reeds. The Brechiners were strolling along the dry stane dyke, some taking a seat on the wooden benches as local children threw bread to feed the quacking waterfowl. It was a serene setting and all was well with the world, or so it seemed.

From the upstairs window of 99 River Street, a cute stane-built cottage, Margaret sat at her front room window behind cream lace net curtains, knitting a half-finished blanket. Whilst as usual enjoying the picturesque view, today she was waiting in anticipation for postie Geordie to pass.

Lottie busily feather-dusted the ornaments and photo frames on the highly polished mahogany sideboard. With her older sisters Ina, Meg and Mary now married and moved out, she not only had her own bed but relished spending more time with her ma 'n da. Humming in tune to her favourite, merry Sally Army tune *What a friend we have in Jesus,* she momentarily halted.

'Ah'll bring ye a cuppa soon Mam.'

Always cheery with a beaming white smile and a joke on the tip of her sharp-witted tongue, she was a tonic. Her dad was up Malt farm helping prepare for the lambing. Her snobby acid tongue sister Agnes was at work so peace and quiet reigned supreme. Today, Lottie was quietly aware that her mam was eagerly awaiting a letter from Winnipeg.

When Ina, the eldest of her five daughters, emigrated to Canada six years earlier, to start a new life with husband Drew and toddler Maisie, a sore void was left in Margaret's heart. She, OH SO, missed her confidante; her loyal companion. But she buried self-pity and swept grief aside, to accept the couple's ambition to search for a better future and escape the dismal prospects of low paid mill work humdrum in sleepy Brechin.

In stark contrast from her pretty, outgoing younger sister Lottie, Ina was shy and reserved, and rather self-conscious of the squint in her left eye and the round horn-rimmed unattractive glasses she was forced to wear. Ina's decorum was quiet and measured which reflected in her letter writing. Her matter of fact news regaled how well things were going.

The day the couple embarked the ship at Greenock, Margaret thought her heart would physically break. It was, in essence, a final farewell; like saying *goodbye* forever. So, when the very first letter arrived from Ina, she read it with a mixture of excitement, happiness and reassurance but also overwhelming sadness.

Ina wrote of their sailing onboard the transatlantic steamer, on a 3rd class steerage ticket from Greenock to New York. The three of them slept together on a top double-bed bunk berth, in a below decks area which was shared with many other families. The rough, two-week journey seemed like eternity, with nowhere to escape from noise and din. Fed on tasteless soup, black bread, boiled potatoes and sometimes a chunk of unappetising beef, seasickness and dysentery over the rocky seas, on a ship with no stabilisers, was a given. Like all other passengers in search of a new life, it was with enormous relief when they spotted the Statue of Liberty and the ship docked at Ellis Island. The passengers disembarked to endure long waits in the queues at customs then followed by medical checks, for signs of TB (tuberculosis) or lice, their Steerage Passenger Inspection and Vaccination Card was approved and stamped. Once eventually cleared, they continued on their life-changing adventure.

For two and a half days, they rode by train with a stopover at Toronto where the local Immigration Hall (IH) provided advice to new settlers and overnight accommodation. Onwards through Manitoba, they eventually arrived at Winnipeg where Drew was given guidance at the local Immigration Hall there on how to claim a free Government farm as an agricultural immigrant. From the mart, he bought Dandy the horse and a wooden cart and set off towards Selkirk with Ina and Maisie in the back of the wagon. Eventually, they found a suitable holding with a small one room wooden log cabin and ample land to grow fruit and vegetables. Drew's bigger plan was to eventually expand the farming to wheatfields.

As an energetic youngster, Drew worked as a farmhand in Angus with his dad before delivering Calcuttan jute plants by horse and cart to *Dukies*, Brechin Jute Works. He'd offload them from the freight train containers at Brechin Rail Station on to horse cart wagons. It was at the factory he met Ina. He was strong, muscular and tall in stature. His fair curly hair framed a rough and ready face which Ina adored. Both working 12 hours a day for a pittance, it was a tiring, unrewarding existence which held no future prospects. Although Ina accepted her lot in life, Drew was ambitious for a brighter future; so along with a sizeable cash 'gift' from Margaret when they wed, they penny pinched every farthing, difficult once rent and bills, including medical fees, were set aside. The voyage tickets alone cost – US \$30 (about £6) each and they'd need considerable cash to get settled.

At the remote Selkirk prairie holding, once the produce was of a sizeable stock, Drew started making weekly Friday trips to trade at Winnipeg town market. Eventually, they acquired hens, some lambs, a cow called Molly and farming tools. He acquired a rifle which was intended not only to protect the family from wolves or black-tailed prairie dogs but to shoot the rabbits trespassing on his land, nibbling his precious vegetation. And of-course, rabbit pie was sometimes dish of the day. Each Friday, he'd leave very early in the morning when Ina would hand him a wee poke with a boiled egg, a chunk of home-made fruitcake or scones, lemonade and a shopping list – which ranged from dry foods and baking ingredients to cloth and thread. Every now and then, he'd pop in to Winnipeg Post Office to post a letter addressed to her mam in Brechin. Sometimes, he'd pick up mail from their assigned post box with news from back home. Ina would wait up for his return, usually very late, in hopeful anticipation of the wares, or letters, he'd bring home.

Selkirk town was nearly three miles away and Ina looked forward to Drew taking her to attend the Selkirk Church Sunday service.

Then one day back in River Street, the Winnipeg post regaled exciting news of a new baby on the way. Margaret and Lottie's knitting needles clicked and clacked overtime to create a baby layette and Lottie popped a sprig of heather in the parcel as it was sent over three and a half thousand miles, far across the sea. When news that baby Morag arrived safely, uncontrollable tears of relief ran down Margaret's face.

Remote from neighbours and the nearest village, Ina devoted herself to keeping their cabin as homely as possible, taking care of her bairns whilst working hard tending the vegetable and fruit plot. She prepared homemade jam from the berries and various jars of pickles, including onion and beetroot, which Drew loaded on the wagon each Friday along with the harvested produce, all ready to trade at market. She was content and very happy and this was all Margaret could hope for her beloved Ina. Yes, everything was going well.

Lottie had by now lifted the colourful wool Axminster rug from the front room and it was lain out upside down over the back green. She beat it, she shoogled it then dragged it over the grass to wipe the dirt from its tufts and by magic the beautiful colourful pattern reappeared. Rolling it up again to carry it back to its pride of place, she heard Geordie bellowing from the front door.

'Margaret! Lottie! Letter from Ina,' he correctly guessed from the postmark.

After stooping under the low lintel of the cottage front door, he ascended the narrow wooden stairs two at a time to deliver the precious post to Margaret. Plonking himself down heavily on the green velvet chaise lounge, he expectantly awaited his usual cuppa and parle.

The china cups rattled as Lottie hurriedly brought the tea tray on which sat an inviting plate of home-made shortbread and fruit cake, displayed on a hand-made lace doyley. Adding a drop of milk into each delicate china cup before straining tea from a handsome matching china teapot, Lottie stirred in a couple of spoons of sugar, then served. She and Geordie chirpily gossiped about Jocky Falconer's new chimney sweep business, artist David Waterson's new love interest and of-course, with a sense of pride,

Margaret chipped in about how well the farm was expanding in Canada. Much as she was fond of Geordie, she was also aware the postie would broadcast her news quicker than the Brechin Courier.

Margaret eyed the letter in anticipation but she would wait until Geordie left so she could savour every word. Once gone, Lottie brought the ivory handled paper knife, to carefully open the envelope, then she slipped out the door to leave her mam alone with her news from Ina.

25/2/1925

Dear Mam

Drew left three months ago for the Friday market. Gave the bairns and me a kiss and cuddle then waved bye-bye, but he never came back. I've been waiting and waiting, but nothing. The winter here is so cold. Garden vegetables are scarce with only the occasional cabbage, tattie and carrot to find.

I've been collecting sticks from the prairie for firewood but with hungry wolves howling, I'm scared stiff.

Last week, I trudged through the thick snow in the icy cold with the bairns on a sledge, all the way to Selkirk, to ask if anyone had seen Drew. Nice Mrs Cotton the doctor's wife took us in and gave us some warm soup. She said there was rumour that Drew had been seen gambling in a Winnipeg bar. And there was a woman he was often seen with. When I cried, Mrs Cotton hugged me and told me not to worry but how can I not? I have no money; the bairns are hungry. Mrs Cotton got her husband to take us back in his horse and buggy with some groceries from her larder. She is so kind. But then the bairns took a fever and we have been so unwell. Dr Cotton has been popping in. He will post this letter for me.

Mam, I don't know what to do. I'm at my wits end. I miss Drew so much. I wish I was home. Please don't tell folks back home because I dread the disgrace.

Your loving daughter

Ina

***

*'…In the depth of thine affection
Plant a sweet forget me not.'*

Glossary

a'	I, all
a' telt him	I told him
a'body	everybody
aboot	about
aff yer heid	going crazy, angry
ah	I
aroond	around
auld	old
aye	yes
ben the hoose	next room, next door
besom	misbehaving girl
blether	gossip, chat
blue murder	very loud
bothy	wooden hut kitchen
brither	brother
bucket day	rubbish collection day
cawing the rope	turning the rope
chuntie	chamber pot
clocked	noticed
combinations	all in one vest/long johns
dae ye?	do you?
didnae ken	didn't know
deid	dead
dinnae	don't
dis	does
dolled up	dressed up
doon	down
eejit	idiot
faff	hassle
fair	quite
faither	father
feart	frightened

Pucklie O' Pickles

fit ye daein' here?	what are you doing here?
fur	for
gie	give, quite
glory hole	slum, untidy area
greetin'	crying'
guffy	undesirable person
Hibbees	Hibernian Football Club Fan
huv	have
huvnae	haven't
hame	home
helter skelter	round and round
hen	darling (female)
lassies	girls
lavvies	outside toilets
loon	boy
luggin'	carrying a heavy bag
ma'	my, mum
ma's	mum's
man	husband
natter	chat
noo	now
nooadays	nowadays
o'	of
och	oh
oor	our
oot	out
parle	chat, gossip
poke	small bag
puckle/pucklie	a few, a little
puff	breath, life
puke	vomit
quines	girls
radge	wild, crazy person
sarky	sarcastic
schtum	quiet

semmit	vest
shottie	turn (in game)
shooglin'	shaking
skelp	slap
skiver	lazy, avoiding work
slunk	crept away
sunshine	darling (derogatory)
tea	supper
telt	told
thay	those, these
tinnies	J Robertson Tin Manufacturers
up the spout	pregnant
weans	children
wee	small
wi'	with'
wis	was
wisnae	wasn't
wu**r**	our

TURKISH

afiyet olsun	bon appetite
buyuk hata	big mistake
evlarlari	lads, sons

References

Poem

Anon, When the Golden Sun is Setting, A Victorian autograph book

Joseph, Warning, lines 1-4, 20-22, from Selected Poems (Bloodaxe, 1992)

Newspapers

Scotsman, The, 2014

Scotsman on Sunday, The, 2000

About
A J STOVIE

*P*ucklie O' Pickles is a debut book of short stories, released by A J Stovie, in collaboration with fellow novice authors. Passion for story telling and writing is intrinsic to their being and they have created this compendium of tales, all based on Scots life. During their Lockdown Zoom meetings, they dabbled in writing creative pieces and some are included in the book. It is their hope that readers will enjoy and identify with the experience of nostalgic journeys and find this compilation entertaining and at times humorous. Plans are underway to release a follow up in the Pickles series very soon. For more details facebook.com / ajstovie.

.

Printed in Great Britain
by Amazon

66050315R00097